Peter Clack is an award-winning Australian journalist and author of *Firestorm Trial by Fire*, providing crucial revelations into the causes of a bushfire that destroyed 500 Canberra homes in 2003. This was the worst natural disaster in Canberra's history. Clack worked in newspapers in Queensland and Victoria before joining *The Canberra Times* in 1989, where he was later appointed as police reporter. He developed networks of trusted informants across the police, fire and emergency services and this opened the way for extensive coverage of police and crime. He realised it was impossible to cover on-going crime without access to inside information from police, and that it was only possible by hiding their identity. This sparked his intrigue in finding out more. He was awarded a Churchill Fellowship in 1995 to study police reporting at prominent newspapers in the United States, Canada, the United Kingdom and Republic of Ireland.

The Legacy of Cocaine

- 1986 – Rapidly increasing amounts of cocaine from South America smuggled across America's southern border, carried via the national highway network to every city.
- 1989 – Massive rise in street gang activity. Gangs have dominated the illegal drugs trade ever since.
- 1990 – Law enforcement agencies encounter record homicides, drug-related crime, gang feuds, shootings and overdose deaths.
- 2018 – An estimated 553,000 homeless, drug affected people occupy roadside encampments in city business districts, provoking outrage, disgust, business exodus.
- 2021 – Drug overdose deaths hit 107,735, a 50 per cent jump in 5 years, the worst ever recorded.
- 2022 – Return to record homicide rates from the 1990s. Shop invasions, looting, street violence – all gang-related.

Peter Clack

BLOODSTAINS ON THE COCAINE TRAIL

Crime Reporting on Famous Newspapers

AUSTIN MACAULEY PUBLISHERS™

LONDON * CAMBRIDGE * NEW YORK * SHARJAH

A CIP catalogue record for this title is available from the British Library.

ISBN 9781528916189 (Paperback)
ISBN 9781398489592 (Hardback)
ISBN 9781528993272 (ePub e-book)
ISBN 9781398400559 (Audiobook)

www.austinmacauley.com

First Published 2023
Austin Macauley Publishers Ltd®
1 Canada Square
Canary Wharf
London
E14 5AA

This book would not be possible without the belief and faith shown in me by the Winston Churchill Memorial Trust Australia. Generations of Churchill fellows across Australia will remember with great affection and respect the unremitting support we all received from 'our mother', Executive Officer Elvie Munday AO (who passed away in 2005).

My loving partner, Sue Whittaker, has helped to keep the flames of our lives burning steadily and this has made everything possible.

Peter Clack, Black Range, NSW.

Table of Contents

Winston Churchill Award

This work was made possible through the awarding of a Churchill Fellowship in 1995 from the Winston Churchill Memorial Trust Australia:

To achieve an international perspective on crime and police reporting in major national newspapers overseas and to compare with style in Australia. To assemble details for the production of a book suitable for Australian publication. This would not be possible without first-hand experience internationally.

My sincere thanks and appreciation to the trust's Executive Director, Rear Admiral Ian Richards (former Deputy Chief of Navy), Executive Officer, Elvie Munday AO (passed 2005), and President of the ACT Churchill Fellows Association, Colin Slater OAM. My sponsors for the fellowship award were: ACT Attorney-General, Terry Connolly (passed 2007), Director of the Australian Institute of Criminology, Professor Duncan Chappell, and Editor of *The Canberra Times*, Jack Waterford.

I wish to express my sincere thanks for the kind support with planning my itinerary from the United States Information Service, Australian Federal Police, Holiday Inn International, Fáilte Ireland (the National Tourism Development Association of Ireland), and VisitBritain (the British Tourist Commission).

Newspapers in the Study

They include the *Los Angeles Times, San Antonio Express-News, The Times-Picayune* in New Orleans*, The Atlanta Constitution / The Atlanta Journal, Chicago Tribune, The Boston Globe, Toronto Star, Manchester Evening News, The Scotsman / Edinburgh Evening News,* and the *Irish Independent*, in Dublin.

Police Services in the Study

Los Angeles Police Department, San Antonio Police Department, New Orleans Police Department, Atlanta Police Department, Chicago Police Department, Boston Police Department, Greater Manchester Police, Lothian and Borders Police and Garda Siochana (Republic of Ireland).

* **Please Note:** This work is based entirely on my own first-hand knowledge, personal experiences and interviews with senior editors, police/crime reporters, bureau chiefs and law enforcement. It includes accounts from newspapers in America, Canada, England, Scotland and the Republic of Ireland.

Authorship

Peter Clack is the author of *Firestorm, Trial by Fire*, an account of the worst natural disaster in Canberra's history. A firestorm burst into Canberra's suburbs in 2003, causing billions of dollars' damage, destroying some 500 homes and leading to the deaths of four people. Clack led *The Canberra Times'* news coverage of the bushfires and he was in the news team recognised by a prestigious national Walkley Award for ongoing coverage of the fire and its fatal consequences for life in the capital.

Part One
Best of Crime Journalism

Newspapers have many roles in society, apart from being mere carriers of news. They are tangible and can be held and read, and then re-read at leisure. They give comfort and help to alleviate fear in a form that is manageable – unlike television's style of crime coverage, which sends readers 'spinning out of control'.

But how does crime fit into the bigger picture of a modern newspaper with its complex subject-matter and commercial nature? The print media helps to dispel the mythology of fear of the unknown, by presenting the straight facts. Newspapers raise issues, such as a black jurist refusing to vote against a black offender despite obvious guilt.

The gulf between 'real life' and the 'reported life' of newspapers produces an impression of city life that has little to do with what is really going on. Or they give too much space to one and make the readers yawn.

But the overriding essence of newspapers is to give people a sense of control over their lives by explaining to them something of the world outside. You can tuck it under your arm and take it somewhere. You can carry it with you when you take your kid to childcare. It helps you get control of your life.

The best of crime journalism is giving people a sense of control over their lives, when reality tends not to be this way.

* From my personal interview with John Walter, the highly regarded Managing Editor of the Atlanta Journal-Constitution (he passed in 2008 aged 61).

Murder no Longer Headline News

Bloodstains on the Cocaine Trail – Crime Reporting on Famous Newspapers is a series of real-life, action-packed portraits from the last golden age of newspapers. The backdrop is set against one of the most violent periods in modern American history. Most large cities experienced record levels of homicides between 1989 and 1995, becoming worse year after year. Large decaying areas of inner cities were little more than lawless ghettos and all these estates suffered from chronic overcrowding, urban decay, disorganization and crime. But the worst thing is that they were also forgotten.

I studied these issues from the standpoint of some of the most famous newspapers in the world in a belt across continental America. I began in Los Angeles in California, then followed the highways of the metaphorical Cocaine Trail to San Antonio in Texas, New Orleans in Louisiana, Atlanta in Georgia, Chicago in Illinois and Boston in Massachusetts. Newspapers in all these cities were confronting the worst levels of violence anyone had ever seen. None of them had a ready answer for covering all the killings or all the violence. Very few homicides were ever reported in any newspaper.

My subsequent visits to major newspapers in Canada, England, Scotland and Ireland, gives a broader international perspective on the phenomenon of crime and police reporting. But it also reveals the disintegrating nature of relations with police everywhere, which ranged from outright hostility to grudging acceptance of working together covertly using unnamed police informants. Individual police and detectives were providing newspapers with a running commentary about the worst of the crime splashes. But in most other western countries, such as the UK and Canada, relations were largely frozen and unproductive. Crime was no longer seen as worthwhile news. I had not realised the extent of this antagonism, despite both institutions being on the frontline of the war against crime.

All these cities were experiencing record levels of street violence from the root causes, gangs, guns and drugs. Police and city administrations were facing a historic breakdown in social order and a collapse into lawlessness. All cities had large populations of street gangs and their principal trade was in crack cocaine and handguns. Their main activities were armed robbery, car theft and drug dealing. With extraordinary levels of homicides, shootings and endless gang turf wars, inner cities were the most dangerous places in America.

As I demonstrate throughout this book, police were alarmed by worsening crime and violence. Those I spoke to were critical of the massive volume of drugs and the firepower flowing onto their city streets. They said the root cause of the worsening violence was down to the gangs, who were recruited and organised from within prisons. Police have given numerous examples of the savagery and tragedies they were seeing on almost every patrol.

But newspapers were also questioning their own capability to report what was going on around them. There were so many killings and shootings that most admitted they were unable to report them with any meaning. None were able or willing to report the sheer volume of the street violence. But a few, like the *Los Angeles Times*, admitted that they no longer reported them at all, other than occasional summaries of the dead. It was shocking to find that murder is no longer headline news. But capital crime did not end up on the front pages in England or Scotland either.

This was the environment into which I plunged in 1995, not expecting to witness such a confronting outburst of raw violence and cities under siege. Nor did I realise at the time that this was a watershed moment for America with the worst levels of homicides ever seen. I had not envisaged newspapers being unwilling to provide news coverage of the killing fields inside their own cities. It needed to spill out into more affluent suburbs or surpass some previous outrage to make it into the news pages.

My research reveals just how deeply entrenched the violence and poverty in America have become compared with any other western country. This is also about the hidden forces that have torn away traditional closeness with police and replaced it with a veneer of hostility and a lack of genuine empathy. Newspapers everywhere are withdrawing from crime reporting as a matter of routine. The once-great mastheads are all in a state of collapse – and police reporting has become a dying art.

Chapter 1
Los Angeles, California

Biggest Newspaper in America

The *Los Angeles Times* is one of the world's most successful, famous and influential newspapers and it was in its glory days in 1995. The paper sat firmly at the centre of all life in this brooding, bustling, spread-eagled metropolis, the biggest city by area in the world. More than a million newspapers thundered out each weekday from 16 state-of-the-art printing plants and it was fourth in national circulation behind the *Wall Street Journal, USA Today* and *New York Times.*

Only three years before it was ranked the biggest newspaper in America, and the 376,256 metric tons of newsprint used each year was enough to reach the moon 14 times (Facts about the Los Angeles Times). The head office was lavish and occupied an entire city block in Times Mirror Square in central Los Angeles and the news desk was the biggest in America, with 1,500 editorial employees. The paper had the nation's fourth-largest distribution network and had led every other newspaper in the nation in advertising volume since 1955.

The *Los Angeles Times* had 26 foreign bureaus and 14 state and domestic bureaus. The paper also ran independent satellite newsrooms and printing plants in Orange County, Ventura and the San Fernando Valley, each with its own entire editorial team producing local news coverage. To give an idea of scale, these outlying newsrooms were bigger than most major metropolitan newspapers.

Los Angeles Times reporters have won more than 40 Pulitzer prizes, taking home five in 2004, the most by any newspaper in a single year – its first came in 1942 for upholding the Freedom of the Press. The paper won a Pulitzer for coverage of the Los Angeles riots in 1962, which took place in the streets surrounding its headquarters in Times Mirror Square. Editorial staff worked on inside the building with police squad cars burning in the streets below and rocks smashing into the windows.

These were the golden years for the *Los Angeles Times* and for newspapers everywhere.

Record Year for LA

Los Angeles recorded its worst year for homicides in history in 1992 with 1,092 dead. This shocked many at the time, but the record was broken the next year with 1,119 homicides. Greater Los Angeles also had a record year with 2,589 homicides, a rise of 8 per cent and the worst year ever seen by police.

The Los Angeles Police Department (the L.A.P.D.) was recording sharp rises in activities by armed gangs, the number of guns on the streets, drive-by shootings and drug overdoses. Crime was breaking records everywhere in Los Angeles (Homicides in 1992 set record for LA, January 1993, *Los Angeles Times*).

While this was a source of endless personal tragedy, homicides were no longer being reported by the *Los Angeles Times,* with its sights fixed firmly on a state-wide and national audience.

Tinseltown

Hollywood exists in the sun-drenched afterglow of the fabulous era of legendary movies and stars of the silver screen. Every street corner and every iconic flagstone along the Hollywood Walk of Fame oozes with the magic of yesteryear. But the big stars, painted-on glamour and buckets of money have all moved elsewhere. Hollywood still has all the trappings of Tinsel Town with brightly lit chic salons, nightspots, and memories. But the streets crawl with beggars and down-and-outs who drift along the famous landmarks looking for handouts or drugs while wearing someone else's discarded clothes.

Most tourists feel safe in these brightly lit streets by night and there is the added comfort of armed guards at every shopfront. In the gloom beyond the business district there are networks of tangled, disorganised alleyways stretching off into the night. They soon learn to be wary of straying into the surrounding darkness, the home of roaming Crips and Bloods.

Squad cars from Hollywood Precinct patrol these back streets every night and without fail they encounter shooting victims, stabbings, rapes and endless gang warfare. This dark side of the Hollywood dream is rarely seen because it's gang turf. Not surprisingly, in 1994 and 1995 Hollywood had the highest crime rates in Greater Los Angeles.

Hollywood Precinct

Lt Mark Savalla was watch commander for Hollywood Police Precinct, and he took me out on patrol with him into these sinister streetscapes. It was a Wednesday night – usually quieter than most – the headlights cut an intense splash of light ahead yet everything else lay in darkness and mystery.

Lt Savalla told me he had shot one man dead and winged another in his years on the force. To him, Hollywood was just one more violent Los Angeles neighbourhood where police patrols encountered shootings and stabbings every night of the week or came under fire themselves. Only the night before two men driving in Hollywood were sprayed with bullets from a rival gang and the car roared out of control into a McDonald's parking lot and slammed into the cars. One man died in the car and the other staggered inside bleeding from gunshot wounds. Lt Savalla said this was routine for locals and police.

The dark streets were devoid of life as we crept along in the gloom. Radio communications crackled across 48 bands and a pale blue lucent glow lit the interior of the cabin. Calls were mostly clipped and precise, but some sounded intense and urgent while others came from further away and were garbled and indistinct. A call came in with intense clarity from a few blocks away; a 43-year-old woman had been stabbed by her drug-dealer boyfriend and lay unconscious on Santa Monica Boulevard; police were at the scene.

Lt Savalla gunned the car swiftly out of the gloom, and we headed back into the lights and jerked to a stop alongside a police squad car. An emergency vehicle squatted like a red tank with its swirling lights sparkling like a prism in shop windows.

Two witnesses were speaking with police; one was a homeless guy in a ragged greatcoat and the other was a local resident who lived nearby and who was out walking his dog when the incident exploded. But he had no voice box, raising eyebrows and furtive grins between the patrolmen. One officer gave the local man some paper and a pen to jot down his statement. Then he turned and offered the homeless man some mints for his breath saying good-naturedly he ought to take a bath.

They said the suspect was the victim's boyfriend, a local drug peddler they had seen on the streets. Later that night a police patrol found him lying unconscious from a drug overdose in a nearby alleyway and some hours later I saw him lying on his back and snoring loudly on the floor of a police cell in Hollywood Police Station. To the police this was all just run-of-the-mill nightly chaos. Fire department paramedics loaded the injured woman into an ambulance and drove away and we returned to the dark streets.

We cruised back into unlit zigzagging laneways going nowhere. There were no streetlights anywhere just acres of dilapidated structures of all sizes stretching off into the night. Outside a small boarded-up shop a couple of shadowy figures came into view moving around a small white van. Lt Savalla yanked out his pistol and slapped it down heavily on the seat between us with a solid leather sound. For a few seconds I was tensing for danger, but the moment soon passed as we edged more deeply into the shadows.

There were furtive movements all around, mostly on the edges of my vision and I was starting to wonder what might happen next. As if on cue, a group of Guardian Angels strode boldly into the headlights, wearing their distinctive maroon berets. They saw the L.A.P.D. badge and waved and grinned at us as we eased by. Lt Savalla gestured back to them in a friendly way but with a wry expression – sometimes these well-meaning vigilantes were caught up in the endless dramas out in these isolated streets.

We returned to the Hollywood Police Station some hours later on a cold still night. The building was enclosed inside a 12-foot wire perimeter fence and a calm-looking duty officer unlocked the gates. He spent some minutes in muted conversation with Lt Savalla before one of the patrols turned up and he ushered them inside the main gate as well.

He spoke with them for several minutes, checking off their names, before they began unpacking the computer equipment and weaponry, including shotguns, a weighty ammunition belt coiled around a gun barrel, nightsticks, spare handguns and stun guns. Their faces were etched into tight angles by the floodlights. The next shift strode out similarly armed and equipped before fitting out the squad car then melting away to do battle somewhere in the soft Hollywood night.

Inside the police station a dozen or so youthful teenagers were shackled at intervals around the building slumped in chairs chained to the walls. Most were dozing, or pretending to doze, and I noticed they all had shaved heads, a sure sign they were gang members. They had been picked up because they were affected by drugs or alcohol and police said they would be held for their own protection and released in the morning.

Clearly, Hollywood was a dangerous place. The precinct's overall crime rates were higher than every other precinct in Los Angeles according to the L.A.P.D. *Statistical Digest* for 1993. Hollywood precinct had recorded 22,652 criminal offences over the year, including 44 homicides (for 200,000 residents in 48.9 square kilometres). That was just for Hollywood but while this was significant enough other precincts were even more deadly:

- 77th Street Precinct had 154 homicides (with 173,000 residents)
- Southeast Precinct had 133 homicides (with 126,000 residents)
- Rampart District had 123 homicides (with 263,000 residents crammed into only 20 square kilometres).

Some precincts in Los Angeles had higher homicide rates than major American cities. For example, Denver had 74 homicides in 1993 for a population of 772,000, Boston 98 homicides for a population of 692,000 and Minneapolis 58 homicides for a population of 429,000.

OJ Simpson

The OJ Simpson trial was the biggest news story in the world, and it was playing out on the doorstep of the *Los Angeles Times*. The story broke sensationally on live television on June 13, 1994, with OJ Simpson filmed driving slowly along the California Freeway flanked by a fleet of police cars and helicopters. It was a stunning moment in police and crime history.

But even though the *Los Angeles Times* was the biggest newspaper in America it did not have a single police informant among the many homicide detectives and patrolmen prowling the Simpson estate. There were no crime reporters on the news desk in central Los Angeles either.

This was a paper with a proud history of national and international news leadership with bureaus across America and the world. Yet not one serving officer from the L.A.P.D. was willing to talk to them 'off the record' anymore. The long-standing antagonism was too deeply entrenched, and no police officer was willing to give important, sensitive background information on the biggest case of their careers to reporters they did not know and had never met.

This meant the *Los Angeles Times* lost news leadership of the biggest news event of the decade in its own back yard. Traditional police reporters work for years to have police informants for just such a day. That day had now come and gone.

Metro Editor Leo Wolinksy

Leo Wolinksy said the *Los Angeles Times* was no longer able to cover the city's record-breaking homicides with any understanding, so the paper had shifted its focus to providing occasional homicide summaries. This meant there was no dedicated crime reporters on its metro desk in Times Mirror Square. In the wake of serious street violence involving police, the *Los Angeles Times* decided to concentrate on examining the behaviour of the L.A.P.D.

The paper ran a news wire service in police headquarters about a block away, which kept an ear on police movements using 48 radio bands. "We generally don't miss much," he said. "At least we *know* about the things that are happening."

Crime incidents the *Los Angeles Times* did not cover usually led the nightly TV news anyway. Crime featured in roughly half of all TV news and cameras aired graphic footage directly from crime scenes. But this approach failed to convey a sense of some bigger picture any better than newspapers could.

"[TV coverage] hits you in the face with a series of violent incidents," he said. "[TV] news is scary. It is produced in a way that gives no understanding of why things are the way they are. 'If it Bleeds it Leads' describes television's crime coverage far better than newspapers. What we can do is get down below the event and that is what we attempt to do."

While the *Los Angeles Times* had lost initial momentum in the breaking story of the OJ Simpson case, the paper now covered the on-going drama and revelations during the trial.

Wolinsky said that to many people, OJ was just another salacious story, but it had everything, OJ was a guy who had unlimited money and a team of lawyers who were considered about the best you could get in the country. "It's got race, sex, it's got Hollywood, it has everything you could imagine in it. But for us, well we're looking at it as an opportunity to see how the system works under tremendous pressure."

The *Los Angeles Times* was now educating people as part of the process of covering the OJ trial. "What happens when that comes into play? How does the justice system react? Does he get as fair a trial [or a fairer trial] than somebody else? I would venture to say there's more people in this country that know how a preliminary hearing works now than they ever did before because of the OJ preliminary hearing. We specifically try to do legal analysis pieces, and other pieces that kinda go below the surface and explain the phenomenon."

* Leo Wolinsky subsequently became the *Los Angeles Times'* executive editor and managing editor. He was on the Pulitzer prize-winning teams covering the street riots in 1992 and the Northridge earthquake in 1994.

Jim Newton

Newton was the only 'police reporter' on the news desk, and his job was covering the behaviour of the L.A.P.D. in the wake of decades of public accusations of police brutality and racism.

I dropped in to see Newton on the metro desk in February 1995, where I found him fully absorbed covering the trial from a room with a television monitor. The trial was taking place 500 yards away on the ninth floor of the Criminal Courts building, surrounded on the ground floor by batteries of news crews and a logistical jumble of broadcasting equipment, satellite dishes and tangles of cables and power arrays.

From the day the OJ Simpson story erupted, it had become the dominant focus of his police beat. But he was looking at the trial through the prism of the L.A.P.D., probably the world's most iconic police agency, and his primary job was to cover L.A.P.D. policy and management. He said few things happened in Los Angeles that did not have some L.A.P.D. involvement. "It's natural that our coverage involves the police department in many ways, not just in arrests the department is making but in the conduct of the department itself.

"I think that is unique to this paper and it does a real service to people in this city. It allows them to participate in their law enforcement and to understand their police department in a way that just writing about crimes would never do."

Newton said the L.A.P.D. had been a focus for violence in the 1960s civil rights demonstrations and more recently the Rodney King riots in 1992. Part of the reason for the riots was a deep-set frustration with the L.A.P.D. and frustration with the verdict, and police behaviour had been 'very much' at the centre of the riots. "Were they too aggressive in putting down the riots?" he asked. When the L.A.P.D. opened up and made its people available it allowed readers to realise the department was a big multifaceted organisation, that did some bad things but also did some good things:

More than any place I have ever lived or worked; the police department is a central part of life in this city. There's been a lot of bad blood over the years between our organisations. At least in theory, the L.A.P.D.'s management principles are very accommodating to the media; in practice that's just not been the case, until recent years anyway. There's a lot of history about the L.A.P.D. and the press, particularly the L.A.P.D. and the *Los Angeles Times.*

Newton said the *Los Angeles Times* had developed a good system, but it could not cover a thousand homicides a year. Instead, it covered the way law enforcement went about its business, such as the use of force, searches or seizures. The aim was not to intentionally portray the police as brutal or careless but to let people know how they went about their work 'for better or for worse':

It's a very politically powerful police department, for many years considered the finest police department in the world. Maybe it deserved that title and maybe it still does. There is a particular style of policing here, a very aggressive style of policing that some people consider very effective, and some people consider very offensive.

Problems in Los Angeles did not involve police corruption, they concerned brutality. But the antagonism was clearly evident and on the streets of Los Angeles, rank-and-file police were referring to *Los Angeles Times'* reporters as 'communists. The L.A.P.D. press office refused them even low-security field information without a formal *Freedom of Information* request. Police were wary of the paper and a lot of officers refused to speak to Newton, although he said some thought he was wary of them. Newton said he thought the longstanding bad relationship was on the mend.

* Jim Newton was with the *Los Angeles Times* for 25 years and was a recipient of national and local journalism awards. He participated in

coverage of the 1992 Rodney King riots and the 1994 Northridge earthquake; both led to his two Pulitzer prizes.

Editor George Cotliar

Managing editor George J Cotliar said the *Los Angeles Times* did not report homicides in the news cycle, instead the paper would provide general summaries of homicides from time to time. He said the biggest problem in reporting homicides was knowing how to reflect the volume of crime news without the paper becoming depressing. Six people had been killed overnight in four separate shootings, but the paper had not found a formula to report them with any kind of understanding. Crime stories sometimes read like baseball statistics, but the list did not give the reader an understanding of the unfortunate nature of the incidents.

Any crime that was worthy of prominent coverage must be capable of conveying something deeper, more meaningful or attention-grabbing.

"They are few and far between when we have a way to report those stories with some significance attached to them," he said. "The more affluent the community the bigger news stories become. That's a really difficult thing to deal with in some ways because life is [still] worth a life. But if something happens in Beverly Hills [then] that has more of an impact on the city than the homicides in high-crime areas."

Cotliar preferred to take 'a long view' of crime by looking for trends to report. Sometimes the paper ran accounts of the lives of all people killed in a month. This was done after the riots in the wake of the Rodney King beating in 1992. Rather than reporting homicides as they occurred, the paper would look at each person and the kind of life they lived to give readers a sense of who they were and what they might have contributed to society.

The *Los Angeles Times* excelled in an OJ Simpson trial coverage, or something clearly defined as 'unusual', such as a breaking story about a mother who had thrown her two children from a bridge that morning then jumped herself. "I think any newspaper in the world if that happened in their back yard, a woman throwing her two little boys off a bridge and then jumping out after them, is page 1 just because of its uniqueness. So uniqueness is an easy thing to deal with. It's when it is 'the usual' it's hard for this newspaper and a lot of others too to give special meaning to it." The story was on page 1 in all editions the next day.

News Budget Conference

Everything around the building was in motion as if the walls themselves had come to life. Sub editors and night staff were pouring into the newsrooms, and teams of journalists and photographers were running through last minute arrangements.

In marked contrast a sense of calm pervaded the spacious boardroom, where editors quietly read through the budget lists before them. Each item had a story outline with the writer's name and an estimate of story length – ten inches for one story, 20 for another. This gave a sense of the size and importance on which to base editorial weight. Editors evaluated the strength of each news item and decided where it would be placed and how prominent it should be.

Stories and images had been flooding into digital news and feature baskets all day long from national and foreign wire services and a field army of reporters, columnists and specialist writers.

Potential front-page stories were at fever pitch on dozens of news desks with urgent last-minute phone calls to check facts and details. Most stories were already sitting inside computer news baskets. News-feature stories had been planned, researched and mulled over for weeks just for this moment. Only a tiny selection of the news on offer could ever be used each day and thousands of wire stories considered 'not interesting or important enough' were routinely spiked. George Cotliar invited me to sit in on this final news budget conference before laying out pages and going to press later that night.

The 'news budget' conference is the time-honoured news meeting attended by senior editors and production staff to assess the weight of stories for the next day's paper, not unlike a financial budget.

The following day's news would be decided by 20 or so senior editors from the city desk, who represented business, photography, sport, graphics and national and foreign desks. Also taking part were editors from outlying newspaper bureaus in Orange County, Ventura and the San Fernando Valley.

Story bids about politics, finance and the economy had been researched, examined and thought about throughout the day, covering world and national events and what was going on throughout California and in Los Angeles. Some feature stories had been worked on for weeks or even months. These were the guidelines for news interest: Is it important? Is it catchy? Is it newsy?

*

Wolinsky read through an outline of potential page 1 stories for the conference:

"Should the story on Bill Clinton run on page 1?" he asked.

"Yes it will," Cotliar replied in a low even voice without looking up.

"What about developments in the OJ Simpson case?"

There was a pause, then he replied, "That will go to page 3."

"Is that story for the San Fernando Valley strong enough to run in the metropolitan edition?"

Another pause as Cotliar glanced around the room, "No… only in the Valley."

Two extensively researched news-feature stories would spill from page 1 as such stories always did on weekdays. This was the reward for having investigative reporting teams carrying out extensive research, sometimes for months for this day.

A daily column by Pulitzer prize winner Bill Boyarsky would run down the left side of the front page, a colour piece about a Congresswoman and her romantic liaison with a male fellow Republican. Three quirky pieces were pre-listed for page 1 and others were marked for inside pages, plus a skeleton list of leftover features and fillers drawn from lifestyle, budget, family or laughter lines.

A news production editor lazily sketched a likely front-page layout on a dummy sheet with Cotliar looking on nodding approvingly. He and the production editor had already settled what the front page would look like, and as far as I could tell this sketch was how the first edition looked when it hit the streets the next morning.

The conference drew all these parts together into an intelligible news structure for the next day. But the story chosen to lead the paper was about the African American woman who had thrown her two infant children from a bridge into the Los Angeles River then jumped herself. One child drowned but the mother survived.

They mulled over a possible front-page photo. The decision was made to lead the paper with a photo of President Bill Clinton signing a $20 billion loan deal with Mexico, unless photographs of the woman in the bridge incident were good enough. The next morning the paper led with a photograph of the woman. "Let's hope and pray," Cotliar said with cheerful drama, signalling the end of the news conference around 3 o'clock.

*

Several of the editors then gathered around the table to talk about how they would pull the newspaper together. One of the editors, Steve Mitchell, told me how the calm of the top-level news budget conference was quite different when translated to the frenzy of the news floor. Mitchell ran the Metro operation comprising the suburban and metropolitan news desk, where he took part in packaging, layout, production and graphics.

But the focus of the paper rarely changed after the conference ended.

Mitchell had worked along with most of the newsroom staff throughout the worst of the Rodney King beatings and the subsequent news coverage, which led to city-wide rioting and fires. Mitchell believed the newspaper, like the police, had its baptism of fire in these riots. All the weaknesses and faults had been ironed out through absolute necessity. "From a sheer workload point of view we found we could rise to the occasion. Some days in the riots we had 16 broadsheet pages produced on deadline."

After a night of deadlines and decisions, more than a million copies of the *Los Angeles Times* went on sale from Santa Barbara to San Diego, a catchment of 45,000 square miles (or 11,655 square kilometres) – equal in area to the state of Ohio.

Lt John Dunkin

Lt Dunkin was head of the L.A.P.D.'s downtown press relations office, a job he had held for three years. Before that he had led the Rampart Precinct, one of the toughest districts in Los Angeles covering only eight square miles, but with 154 homicides in 1994. He said the Rodney King affair in 1992 had been 'the straw that broke the camel's back' and the ensuing chaos brought to the surface a lot of concerns and bitterness that had been building over time.

It was the moment that signalled the end of police indifference towards newspapers in Los Angeles. Rioting broke out across the city, cars were torched, people were shot and murdered, windows smashed, rocks and bottles thrown and properties burnt to the ground. Several hundred police were assaulted or shot at and small business owners, notably Koreans, stood guard over their businesses with semi-automatic weapons. "That incident painted a picture of a department that was racist and brutal. I have been in this job for 26 years and this is just not the case. I think we could be better described as coldly efficient."

Lt Dunkin said that until then unless a newspaper asked for information none was given, or only the most basic police could possibly give. Police now understood their media responsibilities and that the community had an 'absolute right' to know what their department was doing and what was going on. The department aimed to strike a balance by giving reporters direct access to police and the information they needed. Subsequently, relations with the media only warmed after the appointment of Police Chief Willie Williams in June 1992, who introduced significant reforms to how the department was run. Lt Dunkin said the L.A.P.D. had always prided itself on doing more with less:

It didn't leave time for just standing around and talking with people and connecting with people – you took care of a problem and left. It wasn't a matter of being racist or indifferent it was simply a matter of going in, doing your job and getting out and going out to the next one. What people want is a police department where they can communicate well with the police and have time to work with their problems. We're a lot more proactive now and as a result we have a much better working relationship.

However, the L.A.P.D. did not give news agencies free access to printouts and information as other police departments did and insisted they apply under *Freedom of Information* laws. Permission to see unedited reports was generally refused. Problems in handling the media were due partly to the department being so big that answers could not be given to meet newspaper deadlines.

Gangs and Guns

Lt Dunkin said Los Angeles had an estimated 56,000 gang members in 300 separate street gangs from all ethnicities: white, Hispanic, African American, Asian and Filipinos. The Crips and Bloods were two key Los Angeles gangs warring for control of the crack cocaine trade. They were invisible to police on the streets but people living in communities knew who they were. He said the worst problem facing police in Los Angeles was the 'cocktail of gangs, guns and drugs'.

"[The gangs] are there, they are everywhere, there are enclaves all over the city. Judging by our homicide rate a lot of them don't get to grow up." He said gun availability was among the worst problems. There were hundreds of thousands of guns on the streets of Los Angeles and they could be bought without a gun licence. The L.A.P.D. seized and destroyed about 12,000 guns each year, but it was not making 'much of a dent'.

Lt Dunkin said the media unit produced weekly, monthly and annual crime news reports which the *Los Angeles Times* generally did not cover. Statistics went out each week giving details of homicides, robberies or rapes and police clear-up rates. Police had to be careful which details were released and whether they could impact upon future trials. "We can't do anything or comment to any extent on anything that is going to take place in court, so we have to be very careful about how far afield we go on that sort of thing."

San Fernando Valley

It was a humid California morning when I drove out on the Los Angeles Freeway to the San Fernando Valley Bureau where I was met by city editor Steve Padilla. The Valley Bureau had around 110 editorial staff and was bigger than some metropolitan newspapers, serving an area of 1.1 million residents. This was more than the population of Detroit or Dallas and bigger in area than Chicago. Circulation for the Valley Bureau was about 250,000 newspapers a day and 300,000 on Sundays.

There were several incorporated cities inside the San Fernando Valley, each with its own separate police force. Padilla told me that reporters called all stations every three to four hours and asked for the duty sergeants in each case. They aimed to speak to detectives, but usually this was best at the end of shifts so events would roll off the tongue more easily.

Police Reporter Josh Meyer

Unlike Jim Newton from the Metro desk in central Los Angeles, Josh Meyer aimed to get the best crime news he could, and that involved developing high-level contacts with detectives and police responders and finding informants in prosecutors' ranks. He said the hardest thing for a police reporter was to build up 'trust with these guys; burn them once and you're dead'.

Meyer said it took a long time to set up contacts and get to know individual police on a first-name basis. This usually had to be 'completely by their rules' but he did not compromise his stories. It is one of the finest statements about crime journalism I found in America:

My philosophy over years on the police beat is to work always for the day of the big story. That is when those precious contacts come through and give access to key facts and background material. It makes possible the detailed news coverage of important stories and it is the reason why the police round is so specialised and so different. All the mundane news coverage of police shooting drills, women on the force, police politics and burglary scenes pays off in the end. Without police contacts, a newspaper is dead in the water.

Meyer said officers from the L.A.P.D. did not want to talk about police operations and they distrusted the media even more after the Rodney King beating, which had become 'a grudge match'.

* In 2016, Meyer joined NBC News as a senior investigative reporter. He is a director of education and outreach at the Medill Journalism School National Security Journalism Initiative.

Getting an Attitude Adjustment

Chip Johnson is an African American reporter who said he had 'felt the influence' of the L.A.P.D., Police in tougher areas would give locals 'an attitude adjustment' and they were generally disliked and distrusted. Locals mostly relied on neighbourhood gangs for protection instead of the police. He said the American Civil Liberties Union regularly exposed police misdeeds and a recent study revealed that 78 per cent of L.A.P.D. officers did not live in Los Angeles:

They are regarded by many residents as an occupying army with no ties to the community, they have ambivalence to the community. The police in this city, if you say hello, they will stare you down. Most are bullies but some are decent guys. A lot of them don't seem to have respect for the people they are working for. It's as if their job is to suspect you of everything. If they have to chase you they will take a chunk out of you. If they decide they don't like you they will give you a hard time.

Police in turn disliked the *Los Angeles Times* and there was a lot of bitterness because police did not believe the newspaper supported them. They would respond to inquiries by saying "How is that communist newspaper going?"

Johnson was hired under the *Los Angeles Times* policy of employing minorities; before that he had worked on the black newspaper, *The Sentinel*, which was 'closer to the streets'. He gave a depressing picture of downtown Los Angeles as a wasteland without any nightlife and plagued by hard drugs and street gangs. He slammed manufacturers for selling 32-bullet clips and 'fingerprintless' guns. Johnson said the gangs used AK47s, Uzis (Israeli designed open-bolt blowback-operated submachine guns) and hand-held submachine guns. He said five Los Angeles police officers had been murdered in 1994, one by a 16-year-old using an AK47 copy his father had bought him. He used the same gun to kill his dad, rang the police and shot and killed one before turning the gun on himself.

It was a brutal epitaph for life in Los Angeles.

Chapter 2
San Antonio, Texas

A Story of America

The police were gone by the time we arrived, but we had little trouble finding the large purple stain on the laneway where a teenager had collapsed and died after being shot the night before. No one will be charged over the killing because the shooter, a local Hispanic man, had been defending himself. He told police he had disturbed two black youths near his car. When asked what they were doing one pointed a rifle at him and ordered him back into his apartment. He returned with a .22 calibre rifle and when they unloosed shots at him he fired back fatally wounding one of them. The boy who died in the exchange of fire was a 16-year-old who police named only as Ramos.

I was accompanying police reporter Thomas Edwards from the *San Antonio Express-News*, one of the most influential newspapers in rural Texas. Edwards referred to the dead boy as 'the Ramos Kid', saying there were so many just like him with similar names in these depressed estates. Crime in San Antonio had skyrocketed after the arrival of crack cocaine in 1986, quickly replacing heroin, a milder yet still addictive drug.

*

The accomplice had left the scene before police arrived – the two of them had escaped from a halfway house only hours before. Edwards began talking to a few locals, but before long the dead boy's father turned up and Edwards asked if he would provide some comments for the newspaper. The man was a picture of sadness and futility on that cold, grey, misty and now tragic morning. He was a middle-aged African American and he told Edwards he had done the best he could to raise his son in difficult circumstances. I felt so sorry for him, his broken family, problems finding a regular job and how he tried to teach his son right from wrong.

Soon afterwards a woman at the scene told us the boy's mother had arrived just after the police and she had begged them to cover her son's body. Instead, the boy was left in a blackening pool of blood while police completed their investigations. The bloodstain would fade and be forgotten in a few days but this human tragedy had left a family grieving for the loss of their son.

Edwards and I went inside a nearby apartment block to see if he could find the shooter for an interview, but conditions inside were stifling. The stairwells reeked of urine and damp and there were piles of garbage and cartons of beer bottles in the hallways. No one was home, so Edwards left his business card inside the door asking the man to call him at the *San Antonio Express-News*.

On the way back through local neighbourhoods, Edwards showed me where the gangs, some with members as young as eight, had scrawled slogans to mark their territories. We cruised silently through acres of broken down and neglected housing. Rusting car wrecks lay abandoned alongside the streets and a few locals stopped and gazed silently as we drove by.

Edwards said the East Side of San Antonio was a focus for homicides, drive-by shootings, drug trafficking and prostitution. It was also the location of most of San Antonio's run-down public housing estates where downtrodden minority families struggled with poverty, broken family structures, poor municipal services and the pervasive menace of street gangs.

Most families here had not held down a job for three generations and the majority were African American. Reporters and photographers often heard gunshots echoing in the background at crime scenes on the East Side. Edwards said he had been lucky to escape injury some years before when a hail of bullets was aimed in his direction. "You just hope and pray the next one doesn't have your name on it," he said.

It was a sobering message about the dangers of police reporting.

Edwards said he had covered more homicides than he could count and this was just one more routine killing for him. "I see violent trauma and death all the time," he said. "But I believe we should give the reader what he [or she] wants to know. People tomorrow will want to know what happened to the Ramos Kid."

Where Hispanics Call Home

San Antonio is the second-most populous city in Texas, with 1.2 million residents in 1995. But it really is a Hispanic city with rich ties to the Mexican people and their language and culture. The tree-strewn laid-back suburbs straddle the looping San Antonio River in Bexar County (pronounced Bear), a beautiful and unique city, rich with American, Texan and Mexican history and focused on the ruins of the Alamo.

The surrounding region is home to many generations of Hispanics, who form the biggest single ethnic group with 60 per cent of the population. Most are American born but of Mexican descent and 7 per cent were African Americans. The police force had a strong Mexican heritage too and media broadcasts are usually conducted in English and Spanish.

Inside Police HQ

The *San Antonio Express-News* had a permanent news desk inside the downtown headquarters of the San Antonio Police Department, and Thomas Edwards was a traditional old-style police reporter.

Because the paper manned an office inside the police building, Edwards or one of his team usually joined the police response to breaking crime around the clock. It was a tremendous asset for any paper. He made sure he was unobtrusive though to protect this vantage point and he went to great lengths to stay on good terms.

Edwards inevitably found himself in the thick of the action along with police and other reporters regardless of what else was going on. He had been shot at and called on to identify murder suspects. One time he escaped being swept away in a flood, and on another day he was seconds away from a burning building falling on him. However, his main news coverage came from going out to crime scenes and San Antonio had plenty to go around with shootings every day, sometimes three or four: "It's just so commonplace, there's so much crime."

The relentless violence soon became apparent and there was a succession of shootings in and around San Antonio every day.

Police Officer Murdered

Days before I arrived in San Antonio, a particularly heinous murder was given prominent news coverage when off-duty police officer, Fabian Dale

Dominguez, 29, was shot dead by a local thug who had been casing a nearby residence for a break-in. Officer Dominguez noticed the car parked in a driveway a few blocks from his home and he saw that the lights in the house had been turned on. He knew the residents personally and that they were out of town.

Officer Dominguez approached the vehicle with his weapon drawn and ordered the driver to turn off the engine and hand him the keys. He reached in to take them from the ignition but the driver, Jacobo Soto, 18, smacked his gun away and shot him using a .25 calibre pistol. This caused Officer Dominguez to collapse and drop his weapon, which fell inside the car. Soto retrieved the .40 calibre police pistol then used it to shoot the fallen officer several times more.

Soto was sentenced to death and executed on January 17, 2007. One of the other two suspects was sentenced to life and a third suspect was sentenced to 25 years in prison for engaging in organised crime.

Another hoodlum was killed by a police SWAT team (Special Weapons and Tactics) after local teenager Elizabeth Michael was shot to death in a city parking lot. A gang member told reporters from the *San Antonio Express-News* that police had burst into an apartment shouting "Everybody down". One suspect raised his weapon and police responded by firing 17 rounds; he was hit by seven bullets and died at the scene.

Only the week before, the bodies of two 13-year-old girls were found at the side of the road. They had been missing for two days and had been shot dead. In another shocking crime, brothers Evaldo and Adam Gutierrez were killed with assault rifles in a drive-by shooting.

The cycle of shootings and deaths had left one man dead and another critically injured the same morning I arrived in San Antonio. Only the day before, police had searched for suspected gang members for questioning over a shooting on Saturday night. Paramedics had rushed the victim, Paul Delgado, 15, to the Wilford Hall Medical Centre where he died of injuries to his head and chest.

The nearby satellite township of Barksdale was in shock and mourning after the bodies of farmer Neal Jernigan, 70, his wife Barbara, 63, and ranch hand Palacios Rodriguez, 33, were found dumped in a ravine about a mile from the main house. Two of the victims were shot using a large calibre weapon and one was stabbed to death. More than 800 residents from the farming community attended the funeral and the *San Antonio Express-News* featured a front-page picture story of the funeral the following day, reflecting the depth of community outrage.

Later the same week, I was included in the news team that reported how a man drove his car through the front of his own home and fired at his wife in a suspected murder attempt. He missed her, but then shot himself dead. This was considered a suicide, so it did not make the front page and was carried in the Metro section instead. These events were all considered routine crime coverage for San Antonio. However, tragic stories like the triple-killing rarely filter out beyond the immediate local readership to other larger cities or a national audience.

Robbery Leads to Suicide

"It's been pretty quiet, but we had a couple of shootings overnight," Edwards drawled the next morning as we drove out along the freeway, again to San Antonio's East Side. It was a chaotic scene. Police vehicles splayed out along the highway across three of five lanes, which were closed and the area taped off. Sergeant David Ramos was the head of police public information, and he strode back and forth animatedly between the crime scene and a jostling media pack of reporters, photographers and TV cameras. He told them what was going on and gave on-air interviews for Spanish-speaking radio and television.

The string of events leading to the shooting began when a 43-year-old man attempted to rob the 24K Gold Club, an adult entertainment venue in San Antonio. Staff were counting the previous night's takings and the cash was laid out on a table when the gunman burst in. The quick-thinking manager foiled the robbery by jamming his hand under the gun hammer and the would-be armed robber escaped on his Honda motorbike.

Police were called and a patrol car stopped the suspect soon afterwards on the highway. The man drew his pistol but did not return fire when an officer unloosed three shots at him from close range. The .40 calibre bullets pancaked on the motorbike's plastic windscreen reducing their velocity, but they failed to penetrate the suspect's skin. The man then shot himself and collapsed dead on the roadway where the body lay covered in darkening blood when we arrived.

Sergeant Ramos told Edwards it was one more sad story about a man's life going off the rails. He had no previous criminal record, and it seemed his life had taken a turn for the worse some time before this final bungled robbery. His marriage had failed and he lost his job before becoming an itinerant and moving to find some sort of work around San Antonio. The robbery attempt appeared to be on impulse.

The department's 'shooting team' turned up, a specialised police unit that was called in whenever police were involved in a shooting. It was set up after a policeman shot and killed a fellow officer during an investigation into his own involvement in a shooting. This latest incident would end up before a grand jury. The officer involved was from the traffic enforcement police, a dedicated squad that did not usually perform routine police work.

The story and a graphic picture of the body spread-eagled between an upturned Honda and the highway sidewall featured in the Metro section the next day. It did not make the front page though and I recall saying to Edwards that this would have been on the front page in Australia.

Tragic Double Killing

Another call came in. This time, a man had shot his wife in the chest hours before and after telephoning his sister-in-law to tell her about it he shot himself dead. Both were in their mid-thirties and had two children, who were not at home at the time of the tragedy, and the woman died 90 minutes afterwards. I drove out with the night reporter, Elisandro Garza, and we joined the TV news crews at the scene in cold sprinkling rain. Police had closed the streets and would not let us through, so we all stood around in the rain for an hour until a detective came out and said it was a murder-suicide.

The sister-in-law and her husband walked by us to get to their car and the woman was crying and clinging to her husband. When they drove away another older couple walked by and they were sobbing as well. Around a dozen people were standing across the street speculating about all the fuss and a few locals went past on their nightly jogs or walking their dogs but did not pay much attention to the drama of the police cars and news teams. This was just life as usual.

Because it was a suicide, editors were not interested in the story and it ran as a brief in the Metro section the next day.

"We have children aged 12 committing murder here," Garza said ruefully as we drove back to the news desk in police headquarters. "Juveniles and gangs are the biggest problem. [Under our laws] they can carry out crimes until they are 17 and then have a clean slate. That's just outright wrong. Those kids know what they are doing. The fact that they shoot and take money shows an awareness of what they do. They know what's going on." Garza blamed 'bleeding heart liberals' for laws that allowed killers to walk free for capital crimes.

One example of this happened just the week before when four juveniles aged 13 to 16 had gone into a convenience store, robbed it and shot dead the store clerk. The clerk had been cooperating but "They just shot him," Garza said. "There was no struggle or nothing." He said moves were underway to have juveniles treated as adults, making them eligible for the death penalty. Garza did not blame gun laws because it was people doing the killing. Guns had their place, but some people kept grenade launchers in their homes. "But you don't need howitzers and machine guns. Some people go too far."

Garza was born in Michigan where he worked on his college newspaper. He was hired on a *San Antonio Express-News* minority intake program in 1986 starting in general suburban news. In 1987 he began working on the police beat three days a week and in May 1989 he was hired full-time. He had worked the afternoon and night shifts since 1990. Garza saw his job as getting on to stories quickly and there was no end to them.

Editor Jim Moss

Jim Moss said San Antonio may have a high crime rate, but it was also a melting pot for different ethnicities. This mix contributed to poverty, poor education and poor cultural relations. "Put those things together and you've got crime." He said America was going through a violent period in which people were using guns to vent their tempers instead of in a peaceable, reasonable way.

Unrest and terrorism had followed on the two world wars and answers were needed for poor education and poverty, which in turn might curtail crime. Outbreaks of crime coincided with immigration patterns and there were not enough schools and hospitals were under maximum pressure. There was an enormous cost for the health care of so many impoverished illegal immigrants.

Moss said broken homes were among the biggest factors contributing to crime in San Antonio. Single parents were poor and alone and unable to provide supervision for their children and they suffered from unemployment and low incomes, often living on welfare payments. The *San Antonio Express-News* had focused its news coverage on crime year after year, but Moss said he had to get the balance right because over-emphasis was as bad as under-emphasis:

You become immune to it. TV networks and cable [news] show lots of violence, and police TV shows and covering riots are most popular. They make a culture for young people to emulate, and they become immune to pain and suffering. That's a major factor. I'm confident we will work it out, but I don't know the answer to it. President Clinton doesn't have the answers either.

Moss said newspapers were a form of cheap entertainment where reality and fantasy blurred together in a 'newspaper sideshow'. The crime content provided a contrived pseudo-fiction along with occasional blistering photographs and headlines. Newspapers were taking readers into a world where reporters and police had become accomplished actors in daily dramas, and newspapers were a sublime omniscient voice. But few understood the processes at work behind the scenes to contrive the news into the highly polished newspapers that they had become.

Sergeant David Ramos

Sergeant Ramos was the head of police public affairs, a former homicide detective and a fourth-generation Mexican American. He said guns were a sadistic feature of crime in San Antonio and drive-by shootings were particularly bad. There had been 1,262 drive-by shootings in 1993 or more than 100 a month, and four every day in the worst months of May and November. Drive-by shootings had fallen to 540 in 1994, which Sergeant Ramos said was a dramatic change. Only 65 drive-by shootings were reported in San Antonio for the first three months of 1995, an average of less than six a week.

He said youth gangs and 'gang wannabes' were behind a lot of the crime in San Antonio. Some were only eight years old. San Antonio's street gangs had adopted the gang names used in Los Angeles: Crips, the Bloods, Angels of Sin, Ambrose, Kings, Latino Mob and Vatos Loco. He said a shooting days earlier was blamed on a gang member making a gang hand signal, and when it was not returned he shot and killed the other youth. Juveniles were committing violent crimes and yet they were bound by different laws under the Family Code. Sergeant Ramos believed they should be treated the same as adults in the criminal justice system if they carried out homicides or armed robberies.

He said relations with the *San Antonio Express-News* had a direct bearing on how much crime news was reported and how police were portrayed. Police in San Antonio trusted Thomas Edwards, but they were not as confident with other newspaper and television reporters. Most police officers did not like the press and felt uncomfortable dealing with reporters. But he said 'crime sells' and this was evident by the sensational way television presented crime news, features and exposés:

> A lot of the time, officers on the street do not see the media as a friend, a very large percentage of officers. There is a general feeling for all the community that maybe the media can't be trusted.

He did not know if this was just a police view, but he felt the public was seeing the media in a different light largely because of the OJ Simpson trial. Sergeant Ramos said there was a provision in the US Constitution for people to be given information and for some police to agree to talk to the media if they were not identified. There was also 'pressure' to protect people's privacy, so the press was not given unlimited information on serious crimes. But he said reporters could go through police printouts in San Antonio on any day to compile an outline of selected crimes in districts identified by zip codes.

Police could insist reporters asked for information under *Freedom of Information* laws but he did not want to go out of his way to make things difficult for them. He usually referred them to the *Texas Open Records Handbook*, a standing guide to the release of official information containing useful examples of rulings to justify denials.

Lt Don Wilson, Narcotics

Lt Don Wilson said drug-related crime had increased dramatically in San Antonio once crack cocaine became the dominant street drug after 1986. Arrests for drug offences had jumped tenfold and crack cocaine now played a crucial role in increased street violence. All the drugs were being carried along the Cocaine Trail from Mexico and Latin America.

Cocaine seizures were at record levels in San Antonio and the increase showed up in surging drug-related arrests. Police made 172 arrests for possession of cocaine in 1985 but by 1994 the number of arrests had increased tenfold to 1,723.

Lt Wilson said crack cocaine was cheap, plentiful and available. Police seized 216 pounds of cocaine in 1994 compared with only 14 pounds in 1985. A rock of crack once sold for $125 to $130 but the price had dropped to $10 or $15 and it was widely available. Powder in rock form was the drug of choice in San

Antonio and heroin had become a thing of the past. He said many police longed for the return of heroin because of the unpredictable violent behaviour associated with crack cocaine.

Street gangs were responsible for many of San Antonio's homicides, as well as most of the violent crime and narcotics offences. The police department had created a specialist juvenile crime unit in 1993 to target street gangs. It was meeting with some success and the crime rate was 'just a bit' lower. San Antonio's homicide rate reached a record of 229 deaths in 1993. This fell to 94 the next year but then it rose back to 140 in 1995.

San Antonio Police Chief Al Philippus (who retired in 2002), announced that homicide rates were falling, which he credited to the department's community-based policing program and the justice system. His aim was strategic, to lower fear levels among residents who suffered from a perception that crime was out of control when it was not.

Thomas Edwards

Of all the cities I visited this was the closest to a partnership I saw anywhere. Edwards knew there would be a price to pay for crossing some undefined line of trust by breaching a confidence, making factual errors or deliberately slanting stories against police. He would face immediate countermeasures if he failed to balance stories or if he raised uncomfortable questions about police motivations or actions.

"Over the years we have built up an understanding," he said. "The things we see that are non-public stay non-public, in many cases we would not name unless the witness agreed."

Edwards said working inside police headquarters meant he knew which operations were being run almost as soon as the police. He could tip off his news desk in time to get photographers out to crime scenes, but it also demanded his careful handling of crime coverage. He also needed to write impartially on any critical police issues to avoid being perceived as a police advocate – newsroom editors had to trust his copy and be confident he would not deliberately overlook any stories unfavourable to police.

Reporters needed to get close to their sources, particularly on the police beat, and Edwards knew he was treading a fine line. Nevertheless, his dealings with police were all based on mutual trust and openness.

All his stories revolved around visible violent crime and there was far more than he could possibly cover anyway. Police would appear in Edwards' crime stories as voices of authority and sources of legitimate facts. They would be named and give a lot of credibility to his stories. Edwards sought to present all sides of issues since everyone in the department knew who he was speaking to anyway. This worked very well for readers and for the newspaper.

Edwards was generally regarded favourably by readers. He was well-informed on all police-related issues and there were benefits all round. The paper was on top of crime coverage and police could expect fair treatment and this set the tone for other media outlets. Edwards' familiar by-line made him a non-police expert on police and crime, and he also hosted his own weekly one-hour radio show. His coverage was informed and treated prominently but he did not sit back and only rely on the police handfeeding him. He listened to police radio scanners inside his office as well and photographers carried scanners in their cars.

Working from offices inside police stations had largely been abandoned across America after the 1950s, a general retreat due to growing perceptions of being too close to police and traditional police reporters like Edwards had gone underground. A new breed of crime reporters and generalist crime desks soon began to replace them evolving in different ways.

Being 'on the inside' had its distinct advantages and Edwards had little trouble getting police to talk about operations when responding officers returned to the station. He was aware of his own precarious existence amongst them and he worked hard to maintain the beneficial and open-ended working relations. He knew he must avoid being seen to deliberately breach a confidence or show disloyalty.

But this has its pitfalls and the last thing Edwards wanted was to have police trooping into his office the next morning to tell him off. This had a strong influence on how hard he worked to ensure accuracy and balance.

Each new day presented Edwards with tangible and intangible equations about how to grapple with crime coverage and not undermine his own general strategic position with police. In his case, it was an even bigger challenge because his sources usually were not anonymous. They were formal and highly visible and if he made a blunder or reported about police corruption unfairly it was likely to set off a chain reaction. Consequently, he and his police contacts were likely to suffer.

His stories came from numerous anonymous police sources as well, but he mainly accessed 'official channels'. This included the department's public information office run by Sergeant Ramos, or patrol officers' field reports, which were made available to reporters with confidential details blocked out. Edwards fashioned his daily routine around police activities, working and writing from his tiny foothold in their world and matching his working hours to theirs. He started at six o'clock each morning reading through field reports from the night before, assessing the chronology of overnight events and talking to officers coming off shift.

He said the *San Antonio Express-News* was interested primarily in getting the best crime coverage it could, and with police already willingly going along there was no reason not to use all avenues open to him. Crime was an endless source of good readable news, and the paper would run as much as he could produce. Readers would see an insider's account of police activities as they protected their city from crime. Overall, it was an effective way to get great ongoing crime coverage and a successful strategy for the *San Antonio Express-News*. It also gave police added leverage in shaping public perceptions about their investigations.

As for publishing the facts of a case, including releasing information that might prejudice a trial, Edwards said, "You put it out there." He argues for greater freedom to publish because he does not believe news stories have a significant bearing on trial outcomes often months later. Juries were told not to read certain newspapers anyway and to ignore television reports to help screen out comments about cases they were hearing. But violent crime erupted night and day in San Antonio and this decided where Edwards went and what he wrote about. It was more convenient and easier to be on good terms with police.

Edwards regularly dropped into the *Express-News* building to keep in touch with Jesse Clements, the city editor in charge of the police pod, a former police officer who had once been the newspaper's police reporter. Clements was a great sounding board for Edwards – and an ally in the newsroom.

* Jesse Clements died in April 2020 after a 33-year career on the Express-News.

Circulation Falls

Circulation went into steady decline after 1995 when weekday sales were

275,000 and 410,000 on Sundays. By 2012 circulation had dropped to 137,059, then to 100,000 in 2016 (Top Media Outlets). The size of the editorial workforce fell also from 1,050 to 214, reflecting an industry-wide decline in newspapers as they shed circulation, advertising revenue and workforces.

Chapter 3
New Orleans, Louisiana

In Cold Blood

A brutal triple-murder by serving police officer Antoinette Frank and her drug-peddling sidekick Rogers Lacaze added to a growing sense of outrage.

Officer Ronald Williams, 25, was on a private security detail at the Kim Anh's Vietnamese Restaurant in East New Orleans on Saturday 4 March 1995, the same day that I had flown in from San Antonio. This city was well known as a part of the Cocaine Trail snaking along all the major highways from one city to the next. Many officers were moonlighting on private security jobs to boost their inadequate salaries and Officer Williams organized the police rosters.

The restaurant owner was Vietnamese-born Chau Vu, 25, and she ran the business with her sister and two brothers, Ha Vu, 21, Cuong Vu, 17, and Quoc Vu, 19. Frank had worked on security detail at the restaurant before and she knew the layout and that the owners kept large sums of cash on the premises. The Vietnamese family used to give her free meals even when she wasn't working.

Frank and her drug dealer boyfriend turned up around 11pm that night in Frank's police squad car. Officer Williams knew who they were and he told the owners he suspected they were up to no good. He was Frank's former patrol partner – tragically one of his two children had been born only two days earlier. Frank brazenly tried to introduce Lacaze as her nephew, but Officer Williams knew he was a drug dealer that he'd stopped on more than one occasion.

Business was slow so Chau decided to close early; she was also nervous about the earlier visit from Frank and Lacaze. Chau went to the back room to count the takings and it was only then she noticed the front door keys were missing, Frank had stolen them. As she went to the dining room to pay Officer Williams, Frank and Lacaze suddenly reappeared at the front door shaking it to get in. Chau ran and hid the cash in a microwave oven in the kitchen and her brother Quoc shouted to Officer Williams not to let Frank and Lacaze in, but Frank had the keys and she unlocked the door and strode in.

Officer Williams moved to confront her but she brushed past him and headed to the kitchen shoving Cuong and Ha before her. Lacaze was right behind carrying a 9-millimetre pistol and he shot Officer Williams in the back of the head at close range severing his spinal cord. When the police officer fell back paralysed Lacaze shot him twice more then stole his revolver and wallet.

When the gunshots rang out Chau was terrified, and she grabbed her brother Quoc and an employee named Vui and they raced to hide in the walk-in cooler. Quoc watched in silent horror through a small window in the cooler as Frank and Lacaze forced his sister and brother to their knees. Lacaze pistol-whipped Cuong to find out where the money was. The brother and sister began praying and begged for their lives, but Frank shot them both in the back of the head using the same gun Lacaze had just used to kill Officer Williams.

The two killers began hunting for the others intending to kill them all but decided they must have left so they drove away. Quoc Vu ran to the neighbours to call 911. Chau was too distraught to talk after the shock of seeing the bodies of her sister and brother and Officer Williams.

In a cynical response to the emergency 911 call, Frank returned to the restaurant in a borrowed squad car. But other police were already there and Chau identified her as the killer. She was arrested on the spot and her alibi disintegrated under police interrogations. Frank confessed to one of the most horrific crimes in New Orleans' history and she had intended to kill them all to save her own skin. Ha had planned to be a nun and Cuong was a junior in high school.

The shooting was described as a 'massacre' and 'robbery spinning out of control' – Frank and Lacaze had stolen around $10,000. It was later said in court that Frank had a vendetta against Officer Williams because she suspected him of cheating her out of her security details.

Later in the week after newspaper probing by Walt Philbin it came out that the pair had been robbing drug dealers and terrorizing east New Orleans for months. Some police regarded her as an outcast and a 'gangster in police uniform'. She had been in the department for less than two years and people were now demanding to know how she got into the force in the first place. After her first six months Frank's supervisor wanted her to return to the police academy for more training, but there was a shortage of manpower and police were needed on the streets. Instead, she teamed up with another officer from the 7th Police District.

In news reports one unnamed officer said "What's this department coming to? I've never heard of anything like this, police killing police? It makes you want to quit." Another said, "None of this surprises me anymore, that's how bad things have gotten."

It was revealed after the trial that Frank probably also murdered her own father, Adam Frank, a year and a half before. He had been staying at her home when she reported him as a missing person. A month after Frank received her first death sentence in November 1995 a dog led police to a human skull with a bullet hole buried under her house. Police and prosecutors believed the skull belonged to Adam Frank and that Antoinette had murdered him.

Police made no effort to charge her with his murder because she was already facing the death penalty.

In the ensuing upheaval New Orleans Mayor Marc Morial said he was dismayed at the 'explosion of homicides' and he ordered flags flown at half-mast on all civic buildings. Regular television programs were suspended and Morial and other council members and Police Superintendent Richard Pennington all took part in live televised debates.

"This week has been the most difficult since I took office," Mayor Morial said. Supt. Pennington stressed a police commitment to clean up the scandal-plagued police department. They withstood the criticism and the questions and promised to clean the city up and offered wage rises for police plus tougher induction procedures and training.

Lt Sam Fradella told me Frank had worked in the public affairs section prior to going out on patrol and that he had approved her competency. When Frank was recruited two years before, the police annual salary had been close to $15,000. They attributed the low pay as the reason so many police were forced to moonlight as security guards to get enough income to live on.

He said homicides were a common feature of life in New Orleans. "You don't get used to it but the scene the other night was a shock." Police had become conditioned to violence and learned to block out their emotions. But it was different when an officer in uniform was killed by a fellow officer. Events like that started a media feeding frenzy 'as if blood was in the water'.

* Antoinette Frank became the only woman on death row at the Louisiana Correctional Institute for Women in St Gabriel. She was still on death row in 2023. After more than one retrial Rogers Lacaze was re-sentenced to life imprisonment without parole in December 2019.

Deadly Week for the Mardi Gras

New Orleans is known across the world as the Big Easy, the birthplace of jazz and a jewel in the crown of Louisiana, nestling on the outflow of the Mississippi River. This was the week of the world-famous Mardi Gras, the biggest tourism event of the year and tourists were descending on the city like blowflies on a carcase. Life was always 'extreme' in New Orleans with endless street partying and a whiff of danger, and businesses were poised for the usual bonanza in the French Quarter. Drinking haunts and restaurants along Bourbon Street, where they served up Creole-Cajun food, booze and blues music.

Instead of dancing in the streets, it turned out to be the worst week for homicides in the city's bloody history with 21 killed in an orgy of gang-related shootings. Just the year before in 1994 the city of 417,000 saw 424 dead. It was a record year for homicides and New Orleans was crowned America's Murder Capital.

*

Gunfire erupted on the streets on the opening day and several tourists were shot. Police later arrested a gang member over the shootings and police walked him from the police lockup to the courts building, a New Orleans tradition designed to show suspects off to the media. In another tragic twist, instead of letting off fireworks to celebrate the Mardi Gras there was a rush on ammunition in the city's gun shops. Revellers lined the banks of the Big Muddy and fired off thousands of rounds and a stray bullet struck a young woman from Massachusetts in the face, killing her instantly. As it turned out the week was one long bloody series of killings, the worst in New Orleans history. Homicides had already reached 79 for the year and it was only March 4.

Stains on a Map

Editors attending *The Times-Picayune* Monday morning news budget conference were stunned. They said it had become so bad that many families were leaving to take up residence in satellite townships, springing up around moss-draped bayous across Lake Pontchartrain and commuting to the city using trestle bridges. They were seeking safe havens from gang violence, random killings and chronic drive-by shootings. City Editor Jed Horne said "…violence is all we cover. There are so many homicides that many other categories of crime are neglected", adding however that the paper did not shrink from reporting capital crimes.

They discussed how New Orleans had been branded the nation's Murder Capital by *The Washington Post* after 424 homicides the year before. It was the highest in New Orleans' history and the worst per capita in America and possibly the world. It already looked like 1995 was going to be another record year. In the end-of-year edition for the 1994 homicide disaster, police reporter Michael Perlstein wrote:

It was a maelstrom of violence for which solutions are scarce and victims are all too abundant. In 1994 the toll was [424] dead. But homicide is a plague that does not end on December 31. Every victim adds to a family's grief, a neighbourhood's fear, a city's misery. In some areas, death is stacked upon death until the toll becomes a single indistinguishable stain on a map.

The same edition listed the names of every homicide victim and how they died with pages of graphics for the city's 'deadliest year'. Dot points showed where every victim died and stories examined in detail the relationships, causes, methods, ages, race (376 victims were African American: 36 were white) and gender by the day and the month. Almost all had been shot to death. *The Times-Picayune* examined the lives of the victims and their families and friends:

As soon as Ingrid Perry saw the sneakers sticking out of the crowd, she knew the gunshots had found a target. As she got closer she could see they were shiny white Reeboks, her cousin's first pair of new shoes since he was released from prison. "I ran up to him and grabbed him. He looked up at me like he wanted to say something, but he didn't. He just turned his head to the side and died. Donny Bright was her troubled kid cousin, and he became the year's homicide victim number 134. After the body was carried away Perry paced the courtyard of the Florida public housing

complex stunned by grief, jabbing an ink-tipped needle into her left forearm until her cousin's name was spelt out in a crude tattoo."
An unnamed police officer said:

It's like any other neighbourhood. People are friendly, people talk to us. I really don't think there is an answer to the killings. Each individual murder has its motive. Last year it was this project. Next year it will be somewhere else. There's no method to the madness.

Homicides in Housing Developments

B. W. Cooper (Calliope)	12
Desire	14
Fischer	2
Florida	26
Guste (Melpomene)	5
Iberville	5
Lafitte	12
C. J. Peete (Magnolia)	13
St Bernard	11
St Thomas	10

* Source: *The Times-Picayune*

In the Florida estate alone, 26 people were slain, making the city's smallest housing complex a symbolic epicentre of the year-long homicide spree. No other neighbourhood came close. Across the railroad tracks the sprawling, crumbling Desire housing complex was a distant runner-up with 14 homicides, despite being more than twice the size of the Florida complex.

Police Reporter Michael Perlstein

Michael Perlstein said each problem in New Orleans made others appear worse. The city had a disproportionate underclass and a large section of the community lived below the poverty line. Education was 'pathetic' and the economy was fragile:

It is the deep south. There is a lot of availability of guns and it's the centre of the Houston to Miami drug corridor. It's a combination of all those things and makes a deep and complex problem. The number of officers bad to the core is a small percentage of the department, certainly not more than 15 per cent, [although this is] a large number. The number may have come down. I wouldn't be able to do what I do if it wasn't for the good cops who talk to me about the bad ones. I hope I have more friends than enemies.

Perlstein said many kilograms of cocaine arrived in New Orleans regularly, which in turn supported the crime problem. People without employment used crime and drugs to get by. The social problems were compounded by years of having a poorly run police department, which had been allowed to 'run amok', and the police culture was to 'look the other way' at police corruption:

When you see so many officers arrested and indicted for everything under the sun you must assume others are not getting caught and are keeping quiet. It's all shrouded in secrecy because of the blue code of silence not to rat on a fellow officer.

Perlstein gave many insights into a city struggling with poverty and violence, guns and drugs, and made worse by so many corrupt police officers. He no longer went through official channels and had his own web of police contacts.

"It didn't take long to develop a network of sources to understand the bigger picture. I roam the field of criminal justice and work the investigative angles."

Sometimes as a courtesy he asked for an official comment from the police public affairs unit. Perlstein said the police public information officer was 'tight-lipped' and did not give accurate information that involved potentially negative stories about the police. Sergeants working in public information were good to get along with, but he felt they were forced to adopt the official department line.

** Michael Perlstein became managing editor of* Eyewitness Investigates *at WWL-TV in New Orleans in 2010. He was a member of* The Times-Picayune *team that won two Pulitzer prizes: for "Breaking News and Public Service"; and the Medill Medal for Courage in Journalism for coverage of Hurricane Katrina.*

Crooked Cops

The New Orleans Police Department was in disarray. Antoinette Frank was the fourth officer arrested in connection with homicides in 1995. During the previous three years 38 serving officers had been charged with multiple offences, including rape, bank robbery, auto theft, aggravated battery and narcotics charges. *The Times-Picayune* called it 'the tip of the iceberg' and said the department was 'beset by a corruption problem that had devastated morale and eroded police effectiveness'.

There was no hiding the extent of it.

In December 1994 ten African American officers were indicted in a federal sting for protecting a cocaine warehouse. Another was charged with ordering the execution of a woman who had filed a brutality complaint against him and two more were convicted of stealing $400 during a pat-down search. Another was charged with assaulting motorists, having attracted more than a dozen brutality and discourtesy complaints.

One officer was arrested by federal agents on cocaine distribution charges, while two more faced six counts of armed robbery and kidnapping. Another was charged with attempted homicide and three counts of assault, and an officer was charged with battery and assault after he pistol-whipped his own son. Three more were charged with bribery and theft, two others for armed robbery.

Endless Tragedies

The drama on the streets quickly moved into high gear. There had been a series of multiple shootings the week of the Mardi Gras and making things worse the police department was being exposed as a rat's nest of crooked cops. *The Times-Picayune* exposés were led by crime reporter Walt Philbin, who had spent years mapping and building his personal retinue of contacts across the criminal justice system. Philbin was tapping into these contacts to get to the truth behind the triple killing on Saturday night by Officer Antoinette Frank and broader issues of police crime and corruption.

Philbin described four killings the previous Wednesday night (March 1) as 'the bloodiest homicides' in New Orleans history, where the bodies were all found in the same room in a housing complex. Three more were shot and wounded elsewhere on the same day. Another was killed in a separate unrelated incident. A police spokesman disclosed no motive and would not say if there were any suspects. Philbin quoted unnamed police sources saying that one of the wounded men was a suspect. It was an ebb and flow of damaging insights and rebuttal.

Some of the killings were unprecedented. In one incident covered by *The Times-Picayune* two 7-year-old schoolmates had a spat during play lunch and one ran home to tell his older brother, who was only 14 himself. The older boy got hold of his dad's shotgun and asked a friend to drive a car to go searching for the other boy. When he spotted the 7-year-old in a group of school kids he fired, and the 7-year-old boy's head was blown off.

A Single Red Rose...

In a poignant tragedy Michael Gerardi, aged 25, had taken his sweetheart, Connie Ann Babin, to the Port of Call Restaurant in the French Quarter for 'a night of storybook promise' on Thursday night, March 2, (source: *The Times-Picayune*). Michael had arranged for a single red rose to be placed on their table. But as they left to go home, they were followed and then confronted by three teenagers. One pulled a gun and demanded Michael hand over his wallet, but he instinctively yelled at his date to run. As he was getting his wallet out one of the teenagers shot him multiple times in the face using a semi-automatic handgun.

Connie stopped and turned back in horror to see Michael collapse and die on the sidewalk in a widening pool of blood. All this took place in front of a group of astonished tourists who had just got off a bus.

Shareef Cousin was convicted and sentenced to death for the murder in 1996 after a trial based on substantial eyewitness testimony. At 17 he became the nation's youngest death-row inmate. But in 1998 the Louisiana Supreme Court overturned the conviction after ruling that prosecutors had unfairly used hearsay evidence in their closing arguments. District Attorney Harry Connick decided *not* to re-try Cousin, who was already in jail on a separate 20-year sentence for armed robbery. Inexplicably, Cousin was released from prison in 2005.

Mardi Gras Crime Spree

A list of some of the shooting episodes in New Orleans during this period.

- Saturday, February 25 – Tyrone Cross, 36, shot to death
- Sunday, February 26 – three women at the Bacchus parade wounded in the crossfire of a gun battle; Jermaine Shields, 18, shot

- Monday, February 27 – Frank Ambrose, 29, killed his estranged wife's mother, Genevie Joseph, 65, and her daughter, who was 23, then he killed himself
- Tuesday, February 28 – Nathanial Williams, 38, is shot to death in a public housing complex
- Wednesday, March 1 – James Jackson, 43, Ian Jackson, 24, Willie Leggett, 22 and Robert Simons, 24, die in a hail of bullets when a gunman bursts into their home; Gary Smink, 21, is shot to death in the French Quarter
- Thursday, March 2 – Charles Jefferson, 28, fatally shoots Deidra Wright, 26, then kills himself; Bryan Ford, 19, is killed and a seven-year-old girl is wounded in a shooting in Central City; the body of a naked woman is found in a parking lot; Michael Girardi, 25, is shot and killed during an armed robbery while leaving the Port of Call Restaurant with his date
- Friday, March 3 – a seven-year-old girl is wounded when her father and two other men engage in a gun fight in a parking lot; the body of a strangled woman is found in an abandoned house, she had been dead for several days
- Saturday, March 4 – Police Officer Ronald Williams II, 25, Cuong Vu, 17 and Ha Vu, 24, are murdered in a family restaurant; Peter Sorina is found shot to death in his home in a housing development

* Source: *The Times-Picayune*

One of the killings had its own brand of tragedy for the family of the victim, Ted Alexander, who was killed in a carjacking attempt on Monday morning March 6. He became the third generation of homicide victims from one family; his father Robert was shot to death during a robbery at his office in 1973, and his grandfather had died of a heart attack in 1950 when a fleeing shoplifter bashed him in the head with a can in a department store.

News Editor Dan Shea

Dan Shea said New Orleans sometimes resembled Haiti or Port au Prince rather than an American city. Shea, who was from New York, said New Orleans was still a great city, cheap to live in, exciting, and it had beautiful urban neighbourhoods. It was a lively city, but he said most men bought their wives cell phones for protection instead of eternity rings.

Gang problems in New Orleans had a different character to Los Angeles, where crime tended to be organised. In New Orleans shootings were 'disorganised' and this made the city more dangerous and the killings and violence much more unpredictable.

He was concerned about the rising level of shooting violence saying the solution to disputes in New Orleans was always by gunfire. Coming into popular use were the TEC-9 automatic pistol, Uzi submachine gun, and MAC-10 pistol. Gun licenses were not needed to keep a gun in a car and this was a source of many weapons obtained by gangs, they would simply break into cars for guns. A newspaper survey showed crime to be the overwhelming issue of concern in New Orleans and people calling in on an open telephone line wanted the National Guard brought in to restore order. The *Times-Picayune* was writing more crime news all the time and shootings involving children were almost certain of front-page status.

It was night-time and we could see outside to the car headlights from the freeway from inside *The Times-Picayune* building. Shea said the window was made of bullet-proof glass. A newspaper security guard had shot and killed his partner in a dispute over shifts a few yards from where we stood, and several newspaper employees had been shot during robberies.

* Dan Shea later became publisher and president of *The Advocate* (Louisiana) a daily newspaper based in Baton Rouge. *The Advocate* later bought *The Times-Picayune* with plans in 2019 to merge the two papers.

Lt Sam Fradella

Lt Sam Fradella oversaw police public affairs, and he was a frequent target of criticism from *The Times-Picayune* reporters, who said they regarded him and his section with dislike because they almost never got answers to their questions and only approached his office out of politeness. He said 'recent days' had been very trying for the department, but he brushed aside the criticism saying his relations were 'very good' with *The Times-Picayune,* the three local TV stations and several news-radio stations. He kept an 'open-door policy' and made sure he knew reporters personally. But he had to be on guard with some of them because the media was sometimes unfair to police:

I think having a good relationship with the media is very important. It can ultimately help put out a lot of fires before they get out of control. Do we always get along? No. But we do have good working relationships.

Lt Fradella said New Orleans was a 'violent and dangerous environment' and police had to be prepared to kill as part of their duties. Violence and narcotics were getting mixed up with emotions and guns and this was a heady cocktail. To stop the killings a police officer would have to be posted at every house in the city.

Crime in New Orleans was driven by the drugs trade and a drug hit needed replenishing every day paid for by burglaries and robberies. The dominant drug in New Orleans was crack cocaine, which was sold in rocks from street corner cafes known as rock stores for $5 to $25 each, and they were smoked and no longer snorted or injected. Street sales were the root cause of violence by dissatisfied customers or rivals.

Lt Fradella said drugs had changed beyond recognition since the arrival of cocaine in 1986. At first it was a sophisticated habit used mainly by the wealthier middle class. But once the gangs refined it into crack it caused a completely different addiction pattern with unpredictable violent outbursts and adrenalin highs. Crack quickly formed an insatiable habit that drove users to any lengths for supplies. Heroin was far less deadly or addictive and did not produce the same explosive behaviour.

He knew of addicts who would steal $5,000 and smoke crack continuously until the cash was gone. Heroin users had a milder disposition although they still carried out robberies and thieved to get money to pay for their supply. At least their behaviour was predictable.

"It has evolved to much more serious problems," he said. "When heroin was the drug of choice police could understand and predict the behaviour of the mild heroin addicts."

Drugs and guns were a dangerous combination: "It's outrageous [that] so many people could be killed in a city in the United States." The department usually received around 50,000 calls a year and most of them were about homicides and shootings. Generally, victims were killed by firearms and handguns were the weapon of choice. This was to do with the availability and concealment of guns, which made them so popular.

When Lt Fradella joined the force 27 years before handguns were low calibre, about .22, and victims were generally shot only once. Victims now died in a hail of bullets and more sophisticated weapons were becoming available like 9-millimetre or 40 calibre guns with high velocities and multiple cartridge magazines. Most semi-automatic guns had 15-round clips.

He made a point of showing me his ankle-worn .38 calibre five-shot pistol with copper-jacketed hollow-point bullets and he explained how this type of slug mushroomed on impact but retained a solid plug base.

Crime Reporter Walt Philbin

Walt Philbin was grinding out story-after-story about gang warfare, tragic killings and wide-ranging corruption and crookedness throughout the New Orleans Police Department. Some of his stories were published under other reporters' by-lines to protect his informants and his own standing amongst them. It was a demonstration of crime journalism at its best based on his relations with key police insiders.

Philbin had been on America's toughest crime beat for 35 years "sleuthing around New Orleans murder scenes, working the phone with detectives, driving around in a car that never stopped at car washes, his constant companions a back seat full of old notepads, newspapers, bank statements and a hamper full of dirty clothes," reporter Keith Marszalek said on Philbin's retirement in 2008. He said Philbin's one concession to fashion was his seasonal fedora – felt in the winter, straw in the summer, missing only a card stuck in the headband reading, *Press.*

"Neither 'rumpled' nor 'scruffy' adequately describes the mismatched wardrobe of the beloved but intense crime reporter Walt Philbin, a sartorial throwback to the newspapering days of Damon Runyon." (NOLA.com).

Philbin told me of the unwritten rules he followed to keep faith with his circle of trusted police informants. Great care was needed not to reveal sensitive police operations that reporters stumbled on such as exposing and then undermining a burglary task force or a lengthy undercover operation. A reporter who bungled these police operations would have a short life as a crime reporter and soon find his contacts drying up. Detectives were prepared to let him report fully on homicides, but they pointed out what could or could not be released as long as he did not identify where he got his information from.

However, sometimes the cops saw through his tactics and accused him of feeding information to other reporters. "I'd say, 'You're kidding' and they'd say,

'At least you're not a communist'." Philbin said police misdeeds could be covered up relatively easily and they would justify it by saying they were killing criminals:

I am sure without knowing it that in the fifties and sixties black people were thrown into the river by some bad-assed cops, they were murderer cops.

For many reporters this entire process would be an impossibly difficult balancing act. But holding back stories might attract criticism from the news desk and stories might drag in other figures who reckoned the police reporter should protect them. Too far one way and the police clammed up and they had long memories. Too far the other way and the editor might notice what was going on and appoint someone else to the round. Losing the confidence of one or both sides would make crime reporting impossible.

Philbin's strategy was a survival technique. He would be honest and direct with his contacts and not base his approach on deception but on thoughtful handling of each story as it came along, avoiding leaving himself or his contacts under a cloud. He could still tap into the inner circle of detectives and the police culture and stay attuned to police politics as well as manage coverage of all sides of the police beat.

Police he had come to know sometimes deliberately passed on potentially damaging background facts because they believed in justice. Those facts should come out, but informants did not want to be crushed by vengeful police politics or official or informal retribution for breaching regulations. Sometimes it was the only way to expose crookedness or to make sure the newspaper got its facts right but it could also be used to seek vengeance.

Philbin said he wanted to generate newsworthy copy for the paper and be at the centre of the frequent big crime splashes, but he needed to stay there to do it. Any good newspaper must protect at least one regular police/crime reporter this way. One spinoff was that younger police who saw experienced officers talking to a newspaper reporter tended to make themselves available too. The same happened in reverse if they saw experienced police refusing to talk to someone from a newspaper.

Police who would like to help reporters with their stories would break off contact if they saw an anti-police theme developing. Things could reach a point where police and the newspaper became bitter enemies. He said the failure of the OJ Simpson case as a newspaper-led event was due mainly to the loss of intimate 'old-style police reporting' which had been discarded years before.

He said it took a 'particular style' to win over the police as useful contacts and confidantes and police were harder to turn into contacts by getting tough on them. As a result, police and reporters ended up hating each other instead of finding common ground, where they could share the process of news gathering and reporting crime news. It was Philbin's proximity to his police contacts that led to the richness, accuracy and colour in his stories time after time.

He conceded that he could not write as well as some of the other reporters who were assigned stories, which he so often unveiled. But they could not get as close to detail and accuracy as he could. Philbin evaluated the tip-offs for them, then he told them how far they should go and what they should or should not print in order to keep the whole process alive.

News editor Dan Shea described Philbin as a 'classic', a former Vietnam veteran who had stamped his own personality on the police beat. "The cops like him, they think he is one of their own and he gets the best stories under somebody else's by-line."

Philbin has left a legacy of how to get close to law enforcement yet stay at arm's length, and no-one could accuse him of getting in bed with the cops to do it.

Last Respects

Police horses twitched in the dappled light as the hushed graveyard waited for the hearse to arrive. Sunlight gleamed on sunglasses worn by many of the more than 600 police officers representing the New Orleans Police Department and six more regional police forces from surrounding Louisiana and Mississippi.

Hundreds of grim-faced officers had come to the Lake Lawn Metairie Cemetery in Orleans Parish to pay their last respects to fellow Officer Ronald Williams III. They lined up in echelons identified by their uniforms of light or dark blue, tan or green. Intermittent clouds suffused the funereal scene with shadows and sunshine. Flashes of glitter glinted from polished buckles, badges and weapons and black tape covered many police badges.

The funeral service was emotional enough, but it was a police melodrama played out against the backdrop of a blue-on-blue tragedy. The pastor described the killings as one of the city's most heinous and cold-blooded homicides. He told the gathering the land was full of bloody crime and New Orleans was full of violence and he acknowledged that serving officers always risked the ultimate cost in pursuing their 'noble profession'.

After the service reporter James Varney moved respectfully through the downcast police, relatives and friends inviting comments for the next day's paper. Officers from the 7th Police District responded with dismay and disgust and one said, "It was really hard when I got up this morning to polish my badge to come to this." *The Times-Picayune* captured the depth of emotion and loss in the next day's newspaper:

It was the kind of day all police officers dread: a light drizzle, an honour guard carrying a flag-draped coffin and a long dress-blue line saluting a fallen comrade. Many cried openly as they walked behind the hearse to the cemetery. There, Williams was laid to rest to the echoing sound of rifle shots.

* *The Times-Picayune*, Thursday, March 9, 1995

Flags were at half-mast on all civic buildings and citizens were calling on Mayor Marc Morial to bring in the National Guard and disarm the New Orleans Police Department. The newspaper's coverage was immediate and comprehensive. It was the most talked-about event of the year.

The following year Officer Williams' name was inscribed at the National Enforcement Officers Memorial in Washington D.C. during National Police Week.

Falling Circulation

The Times-Picayune is one of the oldest newspapers in America starting operations in 1837 – and novelist William Faulkner once worked there. It was a highly influential newspaper with a weekday circulation of 280,000 rising to 350,000 on Sundays. In 2006 *The Times-Picayune* was awarded a Pulitzer prize for Public Service for its coverage of Hurricane Katrina and four staff reporters received Pulitzer awards for breaking-news reporting in their coverage of the storm.

But the paper was already losing circulation and after Hurricane Katrina it was forced to reduce its editions. In 2019 it was sold to the owners of rival newspaper *The Advocate* and all161 employees lost their jobs. There were plans to produce a newly merged newspaper published seven days a week.

Chapter 4
Atlanta, Georgia

The War Zone

Atlanta is a truly unique American city, dominated by African American culture and with an exciting lifestyle as the Home of Dixie. The city lies at the base of the scenic Blue Ridge Mountains near the Chattahoochee River, the state capital and largest city in Georgia and an urban and business hub for a huge patchwork of surrounding counties and rural communities. In 1995 Atlanta had a population of more than 400,000 and an additional 250,000 workers commuted to the city each day. Everyone was furiously busy preparing for the next year's Olympic Games and there was a mood of prosperity and excitement in the air and hopes for a bright future.

But Atlanta had a darker side to her simmering personality.

The bustling commercial character of downtown Atlanta changed menacingly after dark when many parts of the city were no longer safe. A hotel area of four blocks only retained an impression of safety thanks to an estimated 1,000 private security guards and hard-pressed officers in the Atlanta Police Department were calling southeast Atlanta 'The War Zone'. Writers for *The Atlanta Journal and Atlanta Constitution* (the *Journal-Constitution*) painted these crumbling estates as vicious and unpredictable battlegrounds where local ethnic-based gangs would shoot to kill to defend their turf.

Shops were regular targets for armed robbers operating with military precision and using the latest weaponry and eluding all police efforts to stop them. Reporters said locals heard gunfire day and night and drugs had a central role in Atlanta's worsening crime environment.

Georgia's largest city was being painted as the nation's most violent, fuelled by drugs, greed and sometimes the desperation of poverty. "Crime spilled out from the inner city like rush-hour commuters, sticking close by the highways and dallying along commercial strips. Street violence was jam-packed into pockets of Atlanta's poorest and most crowded neighbourhoods."

This portrayal is based on a joint study of all 1993 crime reports across five counties by the *Journal-Constitution* and *WSB* / Channel 2. It told of nightly outbreaks of gunfire, drive-by shootings and sniper fire that regularly spilled over onto the front pages of the *Journal-Constitution.*

Nor was the paper immune to the violence. There was a sign on its staff entry and exit saying anyone leaving work after 6.30 pm must have an armed escort to the parking lot.

I soon found out why.

Atlanta Journal-Constitution

The *Journal-Constitution* was made up of *The Constitution* – a morning paper, and *The Journal* – an afternoon paper. *The Constitution* was founded in 1868 urging the restoration of constitutional law in the defeated South and seeking an end to martial law. Its masthead proclaims, 'Covers Dixie like the Dew' and the first edition of the Metro edition is on the presses at 7.30 am to 8 am – the Final Home edition is out by 11 am.

Big breaking stories often spill across both papers. There were six morning editions of *The Atlanta-Constitution* in 1995, the first was the Four Star, on the presses by 10 pm to 11 pm each night. The Five Star followed with a few changes then there was a 'Street' edition and a 'Sports Final' after 1.30 am.

These papers were produced for several bureaus and had brightly printed lift-out sections featuring local city news. The urban community paper, *City Life*, was published daily and seven other localised sections were published on Thursdays. The paper also ran one-person bureaus in New Orleans for Louisiana, Mississippi and Alabama, North and South Carolina, South Georgia and Florida and it had a number of reporters based in Washington.

The Journal-Constitution had a crime reporter and police reporter, plus it had a large crime desk with generalist reporters, who were tasked to follow up on crime stories and tip offs. This made the paper unusual and perhaps unique by retaining the old-style closeness to unnamed police informants yet creating a wider range of sources across the wider criminal justice system.

Managing Editor John Walter

John Walter had been at the *Journal-Constitution* for five years, before that he worked on newspapers in Baltimore and Washington for more than 20 years and he was a founding editor of *USA Today*. Walter was a very experienced editor on newspapers in high crime cities. He had developed an effective strategy for handling urban crime and social upheaval while still producing a high-quality newspaper for an exceptionally large and diverse middle-class audience. He adopted the 'middle ground' of crime coverage, somewhere between the perspective of the *Los Angeles Times*, which avoided homicides, and the 'If it Bleeds it Leads' mentality of television and strong crime newspapers.

He said violence and crime were a significant part of the news environment in Atlanta, but the paper usually spread its coverage across the spectrum. A team of 15 reporters on the crime desk demonstrated his strong focus on crime coverage. It was all very modern and business-like, and the newspaper aimed at maintaining or improving circulation and winning the best possible advertising dollar. There was an acceptance that outbreaks of homicide and violence were not really newspaper shockers anymore. However, Walter said they still had to be reported wherever they could be used to the best advantage for the newspaper.

The crime desk aimed for balance between going through official channels while still working to find other sources for crime news. They had to maintain a suitable distance with their police contacts, but this was the essence of all journalism regardless of the beat. Walter spoke about the classic dilemma of crime reporters needing to be close to police to develop contacts to get tip-offs yet staying far enough away so as not to become a sort of police apologist.

"It's a healthy tension but the tough questions still have to be asked. A lot of crime reporters have the same instincts that make them not unlike the police. But it is dangerous if not foolish to be too close to the police point of view."

Society in Atlanta was not split between black and white because the middle classes from both sides shared similar goals. A large African American middle-class was mostly invisible to the media and was not taken account of. They were like the white middle class and in a 'very poignant' position, generally law-abiding and out pursuing careers and they only became visible at such times as when black symphony concerts were held and many thousands attended. "You have to remind yourself they are there."

The *Journal-Constitution* had a policy to reflect the high diversity of African Americans and whites on its 440 to 450-strong editorial workforce. An African American woman, Cynthia Tucker, was editor of the newspaper's editorial page and she was awarded a Pulitzer prize for Commentary in 2007 and was a finalist in 2004 and 2006.

Walter said African Americans saw society being torn apart but they still had allegiances to black life in America. He recalled how Atlanta's black community had risen in a city-wide show of anger to echo the rioting in Los Angeles after the publicity surrounding the Rodney King affair in 1992.

Crime Reporter Robin McDonald

Robin McDonald said the *Journal-Constitution* was producing crime and police exposés as a matter of routine, as reporters concentrated on a flourishing trade in hard drugs and illicit sex along Memorial Drive just outside Atlanta areas that frequently exploded into gun violence. Most of Atlanta's hundreds of homicides each year were described as 'stranger-on-stranger' killings or murder by acquaintances. But the truth is, police and reporters reckoned the majority involved drug rip-offs by dealers or deadly skirmishes in the endless gang wars.

Crime became the focus for the *Journal-Constitution* after its 'Banner Year' in 1989 when the city was judged the worst for violence per capita in America and probably the world. McDonald said many people in Atlanta no longer expected to live beyond 25 and almost all of them carried guns, which could be obtained without a licence in Georgia and carried in cars if they were not concealed. Young people no longer had any protectors in the community either. They faced adversarial police, government, family and church, all of which had collapsed as significant sources of support.

"So they pack guns and turn to crime," McDonald said. "We have a growing segment of society in class and economics." Youths are prepared to kill for a $100 pair of shoes and they think nothing of it. One woman's son was shot to death by his friend to get his jacket. "They will kill to get a fix; numbers tend to support that. What we're seeing is a really skyrocketing rate in juvenile crime – both the perpetrators and the victims."

*

The *Journal-Constitution* continued its bid to show that crime rates were rising not falling. Citing figures by the Metropolitan Crime Commission, McDonald said that in contrast to national trends of falling crime Atlanta's crime rate had risen by 5 per cent in 1993. Rapes had fallen 16 per cent but robberies grew by 6 per cent and attacks by armed assailants by 7 per cent.

"Homicides alone rose 6 per cent – double the national increase and the highest number reported in metro Atlanta since 1989," she said. These statistics were influenced to a large degree by crime inside the city limits, which showed that Atlanta was the most violent city in the nation according to FBI statistics. McDonald said she warned police that any comment they made about a police felony or misdemeanour would be strictly 'on the record'. If they told her anything about police misbehaviour it would go in the paper. However, she agreed in general to respecting comments given in confidence or off the record.

Staff reporter Macon Morehouse said the most violent crime-ridden tracts in metro Atlanta shared three common traits: residents tended to be renting (70 per cent); they were minorities (90 per cent); and families were surviving on less than $16,000 a year. He drew obvious connections between zones of crime and zones of poverty. Other reporters told me Atlanta's poor housing was fuelling the crime and drugs and the city was struggling with poverty, violent crime and narcotics.

The Miami Boys

The Miami Boys dominated Atlanta's public housing projects and were conspicuous in their gold chains and diamond jewellery, usually wearing distinctive Dolphins and Hurricanes clothing. They introduced a lethal brand of drug dealing and their crack cocaine was highly potent and plentiful, and they used high-calibre weapons. Police said they were the most ruthless gang of drug dealers Atlanta had ever known.

Staff writer James Mallory said violent crime was having a detrimental impact on Atlanta's tourism. While crime had grown worse in Atlanta the planned 1996 Olympic Games the next year still held the news spotlight. A series of sadistic murders of tourists in Florida had decimated the tourist trade when armed assailants stopped hire cars as they left Miami airport and killed the drivers for their money and travellers' cheques. But since the Miami Boys had moved into Atlanta there were fears tourists could be targeted the same way.

The Miami Boys soon began taking over the housing projects and running the drugs trade. This provoked a turf war with the Folks (Followers of Our Lord King Satan) and police began running a special gang unit to combat the violence. Before the Miami Boys' arrival, the drugs trade had been mostly small-time and run by independent dealers but now Atlanta faced a city-wide battle for control of illegal drugs.

To introduce themselves to local drug dealers the Miami Boys kidnapped a 22-year-old pusher from the Techwood Homes housing project, shot him in the head several times and dumped his body in another county. An independent drug dealer was shot 12 times as he stood on a housing-project street corner. A 60-year-old woman was killed when she was caught in the crossfire of a gun battle between the Miami Boys and a rival gang over a territorial dispute. Police said the Miami Boys were linked to 13 homicides in 1987 and the increasing violence and high-volume drug dealing made this gang a top priority for police.

The Miami Boys used automatic weapons that were more powerful than anything the police had, and they loitered on street corners with walkie-talkies and guns in full view. Elderly residents were terrorised by their drug-related crimes, robberies, purse snatchings and break-ins. Police said they more closely resembled an organised-crime family than a youth gang.

The FBI had rated Atlanta as America's most violent city in 1993 and a close second for overall crime behind Miami. Homicide rates compiled by the Atlanta Police Department showed a high of 247 homicides in 1989. The homicide rates had fallen to 191 in 1994 and to 145 in 1995.

Mallory said he did not feel as threatened by crime in Atlanta as he had in his native Detroit. But he balanced that by saying "Crime is a real issue here that plays on the perception of visitors. There are still fears of crime."

American Crime Rankings 1993

Rank	City	Crimes per 1000 people
1	Miami	186.8
2	Atlanta	170.2
3	St Louis	160.1
4	Tampa	155.4
5	Kansas City	125
6	Charlotte	121.7
7	Birmingham	115.5
8	Seattle	115

* Source: FBI Uniform Crime Reports; *The Atlanta Constitution*

Atlanta Crime Rates for Five Years

Year	Homicides	Rape	Robberies	Aggravated Assaults
1989	247	691	6,796	9,109
1990	231	695	6,109	9,062
1991	205	638	6,479	8,967
1992	198	627	5,824	9,207
1993	203	492	6,049	9,541

* Source: FBI Uniform Crime Reports; *The Atlanta Constitution*

Overrun by Gangs

Atlanta was going through a wave of armed robberies by one organised gang, and food outlets were being hit frequently. This was the Miami Boys. They moved in near the close of business wearing ski masks, distinctive black fatigues and carrying guns. One or two stayed in the parking lot and used handheld radios and police scanners to listen in for the police and employees were bound using flex cuffs and herded into cool rooms or back rooms. Police had tried to catch the gang by installing tactical alarms linked to patrolling unmarked police cars, but so far they had eluded police.

Major Lloyd from the Atlanta Police Department said hard drugs like cocaine were among the greatest problems facing police. The main drug was crack cocaine, which funnelled through Atlanta in two main corridors: one ran from Florida to Atlanta and New York, the other from Los Angeles through Houston, Atlanta, Miami and New York, better known as the Cocaine Trail. He said gangs were just getting started in Atlanta including Posse, Mango Posse and the Miami Boys. Numerous other gangs were named after their locations in the projects where they were based.

Major Lloyd said the department provided official handouts with all the information police wanted to publish to avoid tipping off criminals. He admitted sometimes deliberately misleading reporters in the hope of fooling criminals but did not inform the reporters of his strategy. One recent example was to tell reporters a homicide victim had died from a large calibre weapon and the press had reported it as a large calibre handgun when it was a shotgun.

"I told the press it was a large calibre weapon knowing they would say handgun." This tactic meant the offender might be tricked into believing that police did not know which weapon was used, then kept it rather than getting rid of it. He said the press in Atlanta wanted to be the first to find out the facts, and newspapers followed the philosophy 'If it Bleeds it Leads'. "In my opinion that is why reporters are not happy with public affairs, the more hideous the crime, the more publicity, the more newspapers are sold."

Major Lloyd said his approach to news crews at crimes scenes was to accept that reporters were just doing their jobs and young investigators needed to understand that too:

I just go ahead and give them something. For the TV, I throw them a bone and tell them something, give them something to report. Then they will leave, and I can go about the job.

Atlanta had 191 homicides in 1994 and a breakdown of killings showed 104 were by acquaintances, 79 by strangers and only 8 from domestic violence. Most homicides were by someone who knew the victim. 'Stranger-on-stranger' killings were the most feared, but most were drug-related; one-in-five homicides in Atlanta was related to robbery and drugs.

* Major Lloyd was forced to resign in 2010 following an investigation
  by the *Journal-Constitution* into his military background.

The Iron Pipeline

The Iron Pipeline is made up of Interstate 95 and its tributary highways from southern states with weaker gun laws, like Virginia, Georgia and Florida. New York and New Jersey have some of the strictest laws in the country and more than two-thirds of guns tied to criminal activity were traced to out-of-state purchases in 2014 – most via the Iron Pipeline. About 50,000 guns were diverted to criminals across state lines every year and federal data showed many more are likely to cross state lines undetected (How Gun Traffickers Get Around State Gun Laws, *NY Times* November 2015.)

Georgia was among the most liberal of all the gun states in America. Kennesaw County in Georgia had a local ordinance that required at least one member of every household to possess a firearms licence. Guns in their hundreds were illegally trucked up from Georgia along the Iron Pipeline to northern states where they were sold at great profit to the dismay of northern police departments and communities, already under siege from any combination of gangs, guns and drugs.

A federal grand jury in Atlanta charged the owners of a west end trading company in December 1994 with illegally shipping around 1,000 guns to New York. Authorities said they had broken one of the largest gun-running rackets in the country and national figures showed two million guns were used to commit a crime each year.

There were 6,500 federally registered gun dealers in Georgia in 1995 including 500 with their own gun stores. Georgia handgun manufacturers had paid an estimated $850,000 in federal taxes in 1992 on estimated sales of $15 million. The five biggest Metro counties in Atlanta issued 13,933 permits for concealed weapons, which had risen by 42 per cent since 1992. In January new gun permits almost doubled in four counties. An examination of multiple handgun sales in November and December 1993 showed individual sales of up to 19 guns at a time. Many sales were for 10 handguns and lots of five and seven or eight weapons in one sale were common.

Court Battle over Crime Statistics

The *Journal-Constitution* was involved in a lengthy dispute with the Atlanta Police Department over doubts about crime statistics. In 1994 the department announced crime in Atlanta was falling and was finally 'being tamed'. However, crime reporter Robin McDonald noticed the department was no longer issuing monthly crime figures leaving her and other news agencies in Atlanta wondering what was going on.

She believed police crime figures were 'flat out wrong' – so she decided to find new crime sources outside the department. Using open record requests she collected data from other city agencies, which revealed four to five homicides, 120 robberies and almost 200 aggravated assaults a week and close to two rapes a day. It was a damning finding. Police were answering the same number of complaints but made roughly half the former rate of arrests.

At first McDonald blamed the loss of some key senior police and a fall in police morale but she could not hide her suspicions that the department had devised some clever way of hiding the real figures. For example, the department said rapes had fallen 15 per cent a year for four years. But when McDonald looked into it she found rape crisis centres were as busy as ever. The police had simply changed the way they gathered rape reports by excluding offences like aggravated sodomy and child molesting from their statistics. This gave a misleading impression that rapes were in decline when they were not.

With the help of other reporters McDonald started digging and found that police had been deleting crime records on 'orders from above'. The conflict came to a head when the *Journal-Constitution* took the department to court and after a lengthy court case, the newspaper was awarded full access to the department's entire taped records for 1993. This opened a Pandora's Box that led almost immediately to numerous other embarrassing newspaper disclosures.

McDonald and other reporters then used the police tapes to create a massive data-mapping project of crime in Atlanta. Computer images were superimposed over maps of the city, tracked and analysed and they showed the geographical location of hot spots for homicide, rape, burglary and auto theft. They found unmistakable evidence that crimes were being discarded as 'unfounded' and not included in the police records. According to the police tapes Atlanta's homicides and drug-related crimes were getting worse. McDonald pored over the monthly police reports on the tapes and found that Atlanta had experienced its deadliest month on record for five years.

Analysis of the database showed that Atlanta was seeing two or three shootings every night not the 'one every other day' claimed by the department. Police challenged her findings at first and said homicide rates were down 12 per cent and even the mayor went on public record in support of police claims. However, in a series of articles the paper exposed police efforts to undercut crime rates by deleting crimes described as 'unfounded' or 'unsolved', thus removing them from official records. It suggested that police were making far fewer arrests and it was having a dramatic impact on crime figures. The number of 'unfounded' robberies had doubled in October, tripled in November and quadrupled in December.

The *Journal-Constitution* prepared a four-year crime chart comparing crime rates for the first four months of each year. "We had a better sense of what was going on than the police did," McDonald said.

	1991	1992	1993	1994
Homicide (4 months)	65	65	68	51
Rape	200	198	176	119
Robbery	2,071	1,802	2,002	1,780
Aggravated assault	2,497	2,655	2,927	2,682
Total violent crime	4,653	4,720	5,173	4,630

Comparisons in this chart are for the first four months of each year.

* Source: The Atlanta Constitution

McDonald led a team of writers on a 14-part series called 'Where are you safe?' to explore crime and violence, saying Atlanta had 'the dubious distinction' of being the nation's most violent city. They concluded that violent crime was concentrated in the poorest and most overcrowded neighbourhoods. Residents near the new Olympic Stadium or Clark Atlanta University had a one in 14 chance of becoming a victim of violent crime. In comparison residents of more affluent Chastain Park faced one in 222, and in Gwinnett it was one in 476.

* Robin McDonald is the author of two true crime books – *Black Widow: The True Story of the Hilley Poisonings* and *Secrets Never Lie: The Death of Sara Tokars*.

Crime Reporter Kathy Scruggs

Kathy Scruggs led the next day's Journal-Constitution with a story *about two men* who walked out of the Marta Five Points rail station having an argument, when one pulled out a pistol and opened fire (Marta is Atlanta's rail system, the

Metropolitan Atlanta Rapid Transit Authority). He missed his initial target but struck three bystanders, two teenagers and a 55-year-old man, who were sitting on a wall on Alabama Street. Scruggs said authorities were still searching for the teenage gunmen. This shootout erupted a few minutes after I had walked through the downtown terminal of Marta Five Points just before three o'clock.

In a separate incident a teenager shot and wounded a 17-year-old in an altercation among suburban motorists, on a dangerous day for metro area travellers. "At 3 pm, Adam Radabaugh, 17, was riding in a car on the US 29 near Lawrenceville when he made an obscene gesture at the driver of a red pickup truck, he apparently believed had wronged him." The reply was a salvo of three bullets and one struck Radabaugh in the chest. These stories ran on page 1 the next day.

*

Shootings incidents like these were happening every day of the week and seven people were shot and killed while I was at the paper. In one incident Ruby Aktar, an employee at a service station on Lakewood Avenue, was critically wounded and later died in hospital. She was shot by Santonio Kendrick, a regular customer, and he was charged with her murder and also with wounding two others.

In another flare-up Tuquan Taylor, a well-known former Kodak All-American football player at Fort Worth State College, died of a gunshot to the chest. His mother found him on the front porch of her home.

* Kathy Scruggs died in 2001 aged 43.

Nightclub Killings

I had been in Atlanta for two days when the Monday morning headlines read 'Man held in nightclub killings. 2 bouncers killed in a hail of gunfire.' Another three were shot and wounded at this flare-up in a local nightclub in Dekalb County. The *Journal-Constitution* reported that bouncers had tried to force two men to leave the club because they refused to pay the $8 cover charge. Later court admissions found that one man had stayed near the entrance and taunted the bouncers. The other, businessman James Philpot, got a semi-automatic from his car, slipped back unnoticed and shot the two bouncers dead. He stepped inside the club and sprayed bullets around the room wounding two more bouncers and a customer. Terrified people inside the packed club lounge scrambled for safety behind chairs and tables.

As the two men drove away one of the surviving guards riddled their car with gunfire. Police arrested Philpot 19 hours later. Club manager Duane Glenn said, "It's something you always fear. Everyone doesn't make idle threats, some actually mean it." There had been two shootings in the same parking lot in the past two years one of them fatal.

In 1997 Philpot was convicted of the handgun murders of bouncers Bobby Grimes and Adrian Chester, the aggravated assaults of Kenneth Grimes, Antonio Dallas and Steven Word and two counts of possession of a firearm by a convicted felon. The jury fixed his sentence at life without parole.

Falling Circulation

At its height, the *Journal-Constitution* was one of the largest and most famous newspapers in America with a combined average week-day circulation of 453,000, plus 530,000 on Saturdays and 714,000 on Sundays. From 2007 to 2010 circulation plunged over 44 per cent and the paper began selling newspapers only for the metro area. By 2012 average daily circulation had fallen to 231,094 ('AJC's spring and summer circulation plunges', *Atlanta Business Chronicle*).

Chapter 5
Chicago, Illinois

Chicago had the most violent culture of gangs, guns and drugs in America, a worsening headache for the Chicago Police Department and the FBI. This was 1995 but the real challenge still lay in the future as violence has again returned to the sprawling decaying and overcrowded inner-city estates on decaying housing estates on the South and West sides of Chicago.

In the early 1990s a wave of gang violence was engulfing America's third-largest city and the homicide rates were among the worst in the nation, breaking all previous records with 845 in 1993, 930 in 1994 and 823 in 1995.

The number of gang members has quadrupled since the 1990s and they are in every American city. The gangs are sophisticated, violent and aggressive in their efforts to take over city neighbourhoods and they cut through all lines and ages and use violence, intimidation and extortion. Gangs are the invisible face of money-making ventures run by 'middle-aged chieftains' at the top of a narcotics corporate ladder, motivated by flow charts and profits and often operating from inside prison.

These are among the largest untold stories in America (See Chapter 12, Street Gangs). Yet in the 1990s, gang killers and their victims were getting younger every year and this was one of the great issues championed by *Chicago Tribune* crime bureau chief Bill Recktenwald.

Dantrell Davis, Age 7

Dantrell Davis was only seven years old when he was shot by a sniper from the 10th floor of a nearby high-rise building. Dantrell was holding his mother's hand (Annette Freeman) and they had reached the front gates of Jenner Elementary School where he was a first grader. It was just after 9 am on Tuesday,

October 13, 1992, and a police patrol car was parked a few feet away near the school entrance.

Dantrell was rushed to Cook County Hospital where he died a few days later becoming one of dozens of children under 15 who were murdered in Chicago that year. The most poignant moment came in the form of a small hand-written poster pinned to his hospital ward:

In 1990 handguns killed 22 people in Great Britain, 13 in Sweden, 91 in Switzerland, 87 in Japan, 10 in Australia, 68 in Canada and 10,567 in the United States. God Bless America.

Someone had placed a symbolic candy-coloured toy gun next to the poster.

The self-confessed killer was gang member Anthony Garrett who said he was aiming at a member of a rival gang when Dantrell walked across his line of sight. Garrett was convicted of first-degree murder and received a 100-year jail sentence. Dantrell's murder grabbed instant national attention and it brought a fresh wave of outrage at the rampant violence in Chicago's inner-city housing estates.

Children like Dantrell were being killed by snipers or by other children or in some cases by their parents to claim the insurance money. His death led to the first street gang truce in Cabrini Green, which lasted for three years. The *Chicago Tribune* wrote:

[Number] 44 you know about. He was a seven-year-old killed by a sniper in October as he walked to school with his mother. His murder shocked people. It shouldn't have. Before his death, killers claimed 43 children under the age of 15 in Chicago and its suburbs in 1992. After his death, 13 more kids were slain. Most of these children you know little about. Many made the journey from birth to a slab in the county morgue with little more notice from middle-class Chicago than the few lines they receive in the list accompanying this story.

But like the classified advertisement that writing instructors call 'the shortest short story' – For sale: One pair of baby shoes; never used – each of those paragraphs describing the 57 deaths is its own short story. Taken as a whole, the list is a tragic novel of epic proportions. It is a tale of a society that – in its fundamental duty, the protection of its most vulnerable members – is yielding its claim to the term 'civilization'.

'So Young to Kill. So Young to Die.'

News broke across the world in 1994 about the execution-style killing of Robert 'Yummy' Sandifer, who was only 11, one more victim of Chicago's seething gang violence. Robert's loveless childhood and violent family upbringing and his subsequent life on the streets featured in 'So Young to Kill. So Young to Die.' by *Time* Magazine, *The Short Violent Life of Robert 'Yummy' Sandifer*. The magazine used a grainy police mug shot, because there was no such thing as a family photo album.

Robert's friends named him 'Yummy' because he enjoyed the rare treat of cookies or take-out food. But he was an abused and neglected boy from a broken and dysfunctional home from Chicago's crumbling West Side. When he was only three years old welfare agency officials noticed extensive cigarette burns and bruising.

Robert and his two siblings were sent to live with their grandmother where they shared a house with up to 16 others. Robert's mother had been charged at least 30 times for prostitution; his father was in and out of jail over possession of illegal weapons and he played no part in Robert's troubled childhood.

In 1993 Robert was taken from his grandmother's house and placed in care by officials. But he promptly vanished onto the streets and little is known about where or how he lived his last few months. Like many impoverished children Robert had joined the Black Disciples when he was eight years old, and he had a lengthy police record at the time of his death on August 31, 1994. It was later revealed in court that the gang had ordered Robert to carry out a hit of some kind, perhaps a gang initiation that went wrong. Robert opened fire with a 9-millimetre semi-automatic pistol, hitting several children and killing Shavon Dean, 14.

Robert went into hiding but three days later he was found by fellow gang members, brothers Cragg and Derrick Hardaway aged 16 and 14. They told him he was being taken to a safe place but instead they took him to a viaduct underpass. He was shot twice in the back of the head and the brothers were convicted of his murder.

Cragg got 60 years for Robert's murder and Derrick got 45 for driving the getaway car. Derrick was eligible for parole in 2016 (but was not released at the time of writing). Cragg will be eligible for parole in 2024 (Men convicted in "94 murder of 11-year-old speak out for the first time, *WGN9 TV"*).

At the time of his death Robert had 23 major felonies against his name including murder and armed robbery. His specialty was stealing luxury cars despite being only 4 foot 6 inches tall. There was no lack of gang recruits like Robert Sandifer in the extensive public housing complexes on Chicago's West Side. Like many poor kids before him and since Robert was trapped by the code of the gangs and he died by it. The blood oath he signed said:

I pledge my soul, heart, love and spirit to the Black Disciple Nation and will be part of it even in death.

A child abuse expert at the University of Rhode Island, Richard J. Gelles, said, "He was a poster boy for everything, everything that's wrong with society and families and the systems that are supposed to protect vulnerable people."

Robert Sandifer was too young to realise the game he was playing was deadly. His short and savage life serves as an epitaph to the curse of gang violence in America.

Killing Our Children

The *Chicago Tribune* launched an awareness campaign in 1992 called 'Killing our Children', and vowing to put the murder of every child under 15 on page 1. This was the brainchild of bureau chief Bill Recktenwald but by the end of the year dozens more children under 15 had been killed. Many killers were also under 15. It was a year for burying the young and by year's end the *Chicago Tribune* had written more than 200 articles about them. The campaign was heartfelt but ultimately such campaigns made no difference on the streets.

Recktenwald was the driving force behind the two-year search for answers and solutions to the deaths of so many children but the child killings just continued, and the *Chicago Tribune* wrote:

There are some records one prays will never be broken. Certainly, the record homicide rate for Chicago, established in 1991, was one of them. But when 14-year-old Alvin Gilmore died last Monday night that record was smashed. Alvin was Chicago's 928th homicide victim of 1992. Particularly tragic, is that he was one of 57 children under the age of 15 who were murdered in the Chicago area.

In today's news pages, the *Tribune* launches a reporting project that will detail the murders of all children in 1993 in the Chicago area and will examine the causes and effects of violence against children. By itself, however, the shooting of Alvin Gilmore tells a significant part of the story behind the startling rise in killings in America (922 Homicides made 1991 a year to forget, *Chicago Tribune).*

An increasing number of children were among the killers and victims on the dangerous streets of Chicago and 1994 became the worst year for homicides in the city's history, with 930 killings. The loss of so many young children had become an issue of widespread horror in Chicago.

The new campaign was called 'Saving our Children: The Search for Solutions'. It set out to analyse the backgrounds of child victims and the interplay of the families, welfare agencies and the police. Visible depth of insight and emotion was poured into the project from reporters on the *Chicago Tribune's* crime desk drawing in writers from all areas of the paper. It was clear to all that the killers and victims were getting younger. Coupled with the record homicide rate and endless gang shootouts and injuries the deaths of so many children were now seen as a citywide crisis.

Further newspaper probing highlighted the work of child welfare and support agencies, family support mechanisms, the level of child abuse, teenage single mothers and the influence of young men abandoning young families. No stone was left unturned from pregnancy and abortions to condom use. Research revealed that the Department of Children and Family Services had been forced to become 'parents' to 40,000 Chicago children from dysfunctional families. But it did not make a difference in the end. "In one sense the year ended where it began…" the paper reflected, "…with a death toll."

Getting Younger

Bureau Chief Bill Recktenwald said some newspapers took pride in exploring crime as a news event, like a torn flag run-up after a battle. But the concept of newsworthiness was the key. Small elites of newspaper professionals rose to become the news decision-makers, yet their backgrounds were almost exclusively from the same environment they now presided over. Their ideas were reinforced by fellow editors and bureau chiefs, and this made it impossible to find new perspectives on the way violent crime was being reported.

Whenever he thought he had seen the worst possible something else happened to surpass it. One example that sprang to mind concerned the tragedy of five-year-old Eric Morse who was dangled from a 14th-floor window and then dropped to his death by two children, one aged 10 and the other 11, because he wouldn't steal candy for them.

Chicago Police Department statistics for 1993 showed several worrying trends, confirming concerns raised by the *Chicago Tribune* that killers and their victims were getting younger. Of 845 homicides in 1993, 329 killers were 20 or younger and 92 were 17 or younger. Details on ethnicity showed 598 killers and 353 of the victims (68 of them female) were African Americans, 141 were Hispanics and 43 were white but of mixed ethnicity. Of all the killings 21 were double homicides, four were triple homicides and two were quadruple homicides. There were 278 homicides from 1993 that were still unsolved in 1995. In 1994, 67 children aged under 15 were murdered.

South Side of Chicago

Recktenwald took me out on a grand tour of the Robert Taylor Homes, the biggest housing complex in America. We cruised slowly past these stark crumbling estates on Chicago's South Side in his eye-catching white Pontiac, while gang lookouts were sizing us up for a carjacking. He would not be stopping the car to find out in these neighbourhoods.

I counted at least a dozen teenagers crowded into the ground floor entrances to most of the buildings. They all seemed to be younger than 14 and their poorly fitting over-sized denim jeans spilled untidily onto the ground. Yet these boys were the law around here and they decided who got in and who didn't, and no one was arguing. This was my first glimpse of Chicago.

Tens of thousands of impoverished minority families were crammed into this inadequate, substandard housing estate, a total of 28 separate 16-storey buildings sweeping the cloudy skyline as we drove slowly by. There was no end to them. Each building bore the scars of bullet strikes like a scene out of Berlin at the close of World War II. Many buildings were boarded up and spilled garbage drifted in the streets and the entire area gave the impression of being abandoned or forgotten. Children as young as eight were being drawn into the gangs that dominated life on these estates.

All the building facades, street signs and public structures were sprayed with scrawled gang messages and graffiti. They identified which gangs controlled the buildings and warned outsiders and rival gangs to stay out. Locals had to be streetwise to survive here and most understood gang signs and hand signals. There were many housing estates like this one in Chicago's inner-city neighbourhoods, all off-limits to outsiders, especially at night when potential victims could expect to be jostled somewhere along 47th Street, robbed and probably shot and found among the corpses the next morning. Even police officers said they were unsafe here and were frequent targets of sniper fire from the upper stories.

On a single weekend in 1994, 28 victims were shot and killed around this estate alone and 26 were gang-related according to police records. On another weekend more than 300 separate shooting incidents were reported to police around the Robert Taylor Homes.

Ironically these depressed, overcrowded and toxic buildings were minutes from the luxury and money of Chicago's Magnificent Mile and Saks Fifth Avenue. The South Side is world-famous for blues music, glamour, top-line restaurants, famous entertainers, corporate headquarters, government offices, museums, banks, arts, glitz and elegant fashion.

More relevantly for Chicago police these violent districts were close by two of the country's best trauma response and research hospitals, Mount Sinai Hospital and Cook County Hospital. Chicago has five such major trauma hospitals and police are thankful for them because of the endless cycle of gunshot victims across all these depressed neighbourhoods.

The Robert Taylor Homes were built in 1962 to provide 4,415 separate family units for 11,000 residents but at its height 27,000 were crammed in. Around 96 per cent of residents were African American and 40 per cent of all households were single-parent female-headed families. Chicago's public housing was owned and managed by the Chicago Housing Authority – but gangs are the real 'de facto' owners. They fired routinely into rival gangs' buildings in bitter feuds leaving trails of tragedy and injury and creating a state of fear. At one stage the Chicago Police Department ordered every second building to be evacuated, shut down and boarded up because of the constant sniper fire and the steady stream of dead and injured. Identical problems plagued all large public housing projects across the South Side.

A decision was made in 1993 to replace the Robert Taylor Homes with low-rise buildings, designed for a mixed-income community partly funded by a federal grant. The last building was demolished on March 8, 2007 (reference: Wikipedia).

Fighting for *Macho Hubris*

We dipped through an underpass and entered Pilsen, a district named by the Czechoslovakian immigrants who founded it decades before. But they were long gone and only the name remained. It was still a foreign enclave though, but all the shop signs were in Spanish. Few residents here speak English as their first language and all life is dominated by street gangs, there were 22 gangs in this quarter alone. Unlike the African American gangs across the street Pilsen's were mostly Latinos or downtrodden whites of mixed ethnicity. They fought each other endlessly over gang territory, out of *macho hubris* or for control of the markets in crack cocaine, prostitution and illegal guns.

Recktenwald slowed the Pontiac near a primary school to point out a trail of bullet holes stitched in an arc above the windows. Each bullet strike had been repaired with a pale-coloured round plastic patch. We passed through an area demolished during the Martin Luther King riots 27 years before (in 1968) and never rebuilt. Walls had collapsed and turned to rubble and floors were a sagging disorder of cement blocks, plaster and masonry. It was an abandoned, decaying yet history-making lost corner of America.

Our Day Begins When Your Day Ends

This was the slogan on T-shirts worn by homicide squad detectives in Area Four, for good reason as I soon found out. Area Four had the second-highest homicide rate per capita in America in 1994; Gary, Indiana the highest. Area Four had 210 murders and another 1,065 shot and wounded, plus 265 drive-by shootings, which was worse than a major city like Atlanta, which had 194 homicides in the same year. A further 43 people were shot and killed in the first three months of 1995.

Crime Commander John Kozaritz was the officer in charge on the West Side of Chicago where every day was more difficult than the last. The Chicago Police

Department regarded it as the most dangerous police district in America and where police patrols routinely came across corpses in twos and threes. It was extremely violent and highly ethnically diverse and home to Chicago's biggest concentration of street gangs.

Area Four had 128 operational police, a fraction of the 12,000-strong Chicago Police Department. To give a sense of perspective the Hollywood Police Precinct in Los Angeles had 200 officers yet only 44 murders in 1994. Commander Kozaritz said the homicide rate would be far worse if it wasn't for the proximity of Mount Sinai and Cook County trauma hospitals. "Thank God we've got those hospitals here," he told me one day in March 1995.

Each individual homicide in Area Four appeared in a monthly crime digest as a single black dot on a map, which formed a dark granular stain all the way along the West Side's sprawling public housing estates. Commander Kozaritz said the narcotics trade was directly related to the dots on his killing chart. Gangs vying for control of the streets were almost fully responsible for the shootings, counter-shootings and retaliations.

Police in Area Four arrested so many offenders that all the prison accommodation was full. Around 9,000 felons were already locked up in the local prison with 1,500 in one building. Because of the overcrowding drug offenders were being released under their own signatures the same day they were arrested, even before officers had finished writing up the paperwork.

Detectives were routinely called out to double and triple homicides and offenders had access to sophisticated weapons, assault rifles, Tech 9s, Uzis and 30-round semi-automatics. Not surprisingly police in Area Four shot a lot of suspects. They shot and killed 20 in 1994 alone.

'Too High to Die'

Just the week before two police officers on patrol were fired on by a man later found to be high on crack cocaine. The officers fired back and hit him with eight dummy-headed copper-jacketed .38 slugs but he kept on coming. They figured their assailant must have been wearing body armour or a bullet-proof vest. Eventually he dropped but not before the two officers had received life-threatening injuries: one had the ball of his hip shattered; the other had six bullet entry points down his left side. When they recovered from their injuries the officers said their attacker was pumped so full of drugs he was 'too high to die'. Incidents like this were routine on the West Side.

Public affairs officer Patrick Camden said he was not sure the availability of firearms was the only cause of the high homicide rates. Yet he could not understand how the value of a human life was of so little consequence. The blatant disregard for life was 'scary'. "When did we lose the sanctity of human life?" The rise in multiple gunshots on individuals in street shootings was a bigger question. Some years earlier a victim would be shot once or twice but by 1995 they were receiving multiple bullet strikes from semi-automatic weapons. Officer Camden, like millions of his fellow Americans, said he was strongly opposed to banning guns saying he believed in the right to bear arms under the Second Amendment.

Moving into Television

Editor Howard Tyner said the *Chicago Tribune* was breaking new ground in newspapers and was competing directly with TV stations to give another perspective to crime reporting. TV was redefining what the newspaper did as a news media organisation and in many ways the *Chicago Tribune* was pioneering newspaper moves into the computer and information age.

Tribune Media, the owner of the *Chicago Tribune*, was running the fourth-biggest television company in America with eight television stations and six newspapers. Tribune had introduced a 24-hour television news channel, CLT (*Chicagoland Television)* becoming the first newspaper in the world to add a television arm to complement its press operations. "I'll bet you won't find another newspaper editor in the United States with a TV camera outside his office," Tyner said to me with an ironic grin.

The paper was expanding, creating a new *Washington Post* bureau to bring together all the different Tribune Media newspapers and with a television and print editor sitting side by side. Photographers were going out on assignment carrying Super 8 video cameras taking still shots plus video footage. They would drop in a video cassette when they returned to the newsroom and then it was transmitted to Tribune Media's TV station at Oakwood. The same photographs were uploaded on computer and used multiple times. "You gather the information once, sort it once and distribute it," Tyner said. "You develop a breed of journalists with ability in different media."

* In 2001 Howard Tyner was awarded the George Beveridge Editor of the Year Award from the National Press Foundation.

'Brilliant' Bill Recktenwald

Chicago bureau chief Bill Recktenwald was a distinguished American investigative journalist, a lecturer in crime journalism and a Pulitzer prize finalist on multiple occasions. He began his career as an investigator for Cook County's attorney-general's office, and later he moved to the news desk of the *Chicago Tribune* where I met him in 1995. He was acting crime bureau chief and was leading newspaper crime teams in exposés of a wave of child homicides – 60 children aged under 12 were murdered in one year.

In his early career Recktenwald had gone undercover in bars and taverns across the city to get information for illegal gambling probes. He later posed as a hospital attendant for a series of reports on private ambulance companies, and again two years later for a series on voter fraud.

His best-known work came in 1978, by posing as a bartender in the Mirage Tavern. The investigation was carried out as a collaboration between the *Chicago Sun-News* and Better Government Association, where Recktenwald was then chief investigator. Recktenwald and three journalists bought the building the tavern was in, installed cameras and posed as the tavern's owners. Inspector after inspector came to the bar expecting to be paid-off to keep the place 'in business.'

The investigation detailed how corrupt some city officials were and resulted in numerous charges and firings all the way up to state level.

Recktenwald wrote for nearly every section of the *Chicago Tribune* over his 40-year newspaper career and he made it his job to help newcomers learn the ropes of the newsroom.

Crusading journalists such as Recktenwald embody the power of journalism to inform the public, strengthen civil society and create conditions for reform. The same can be said about the field of journalism to which he devoted his career, which included decades of work and mentoring of young reporters at the *Chicago Tribune.*

One of his fellow journalists said, "Newspapers at their best are not flashy or fake, they are serious about their work, meticulous about facts and incensed about corruption, ineptitude, and inequity." After a storied newspaper career Recktenwald went on to teach journalism at Southern Illinois University in 1999.

He did all this, despite being dyslexic and never earning a college degree himself.

* Recktenwald, 79, died in 2021 shortly after retiring from the university. A graduate of the SIUC School of Journalism, Geoff Ritter, wrote a book on his life, *Reck Undercover, The Many Lives of William A. Recktenwald.*

Return to High Death Tolls

Violent crime continues to dominate life in Chicago in 2023 and the record homicides from the early 1990s are returning. There were 762 homicides in 2016, which was the highest for two decades and more than the combined total of New York (with 334) and Los Angeles (294). In January 2017, *CBS News* reported that "The numbers are staggering, even for those who followed the steady accounts of weekends ending with dozens of shootings and monthly death tolls that hadn't been seen in years. The increase in homicides compared to 2015, when 485 were reported, is the largest spike in 60 years," (*Chicago saw more 2016 murders than NYC, LA combined,* CBS News). Troubles plaguing Chicago's crime-ridden West Side are back in force.

On Sunday August 4, 2019, Mount Sinai Hospital was forced to stop admitting shooting victims because it had reached capacity. The hospital was already treating 12 critical trauma patients following a series of multi-victim shooting incidents on Chicago's West Side stemming from gang conflict (Chicago Hospital Stops Accepting patients... *MailOnline,* August 5, 2019)

Police were recording an average of 15,000 shootings and 23,000 armed robberies every year driven by the entrenched illegal drugs problem and armed gangs. Giving a sense of the historic scale of the ongoing tragedy Chicago recorded a total of 22,046 homicides over a 30-year period (from 1965 to 1994) and handguns were used in 10,772 of the killings, roughly half.

More recently, on May 31, 2020 there were 18 murders in Chicago on one day (plus 78 people wounded in shootings). It was the deadliest day in 60 years. There were 440 homicides from January to the end of June 2020, a 52 per cent increase from the same period in 2019 (which saw 290 homicides). The number of shooting victims in the same period increased by 51 per cent (from 1,480 to 2,240) and shooting incidents themselves rose 47 per cent from 1,210 to 1,783, (shows, Fox News, August 2020).

President Donald Trump told *Fox News* host Sean Hannity, "Chicago is an example, it's worse than Afghanistan. [For] these cities... it's like living in hell" (Violence in Chicago... *Fox News,* June 2020).

It was clear even in the early 1990s that killers and victims were getting younger too and the number of teenagers using guns had already tripled by 1994. Making everything worse, drugs of all kinds but principally crack cocaine were flooding into the city along the various highways making up the Cocaine Trail. In more recent years the dominant form of drugs is from the opioid family, mainly fentanyl, which is manufactured in Chinese laboratories.

Falling Circulation

The *Chicago Tribune* was the fifth highest-selling newspaper in America in 1995 behind the *Los Angeles Times*. It had a week-day circulation of 750,000 copies rising to 1.3 million on Sundays. Circulation began falling after 2000 and by 2018 week-day circulation had dropped to 448,930, 331,190 on Saturdays and 853,324 on Sundays. The *Chicago Tribune* was still a major influential American newspaper, but circulation was falling dramatically.

Chapter 6
Boston, Massachusetts

Editor Matthew Storin

Matthew Storin said the *Boston Globe* wanted to avoid 'blanket coverage' of crime and violence in every edition.

He said television news was dominated by crime but this approach failed to give context or explanations for the underlying social issues that contribute to crime. This is what the *Boston Globe* tried to do. He said Boston's middle-class suburbs were considered to be safe at night and that most of the street crime was in poorer areas, and usually involved people who knew each other – code for gangs, the illicit drug trade or violence associated with guns. He said the randomness of street crime created a sense of fear in the community, but instances of people being murdered were largely about being "in the wrong place at the wrong time".

The paper covered as much crime as it could, however, adding opinion and analysis and reporting later court cases in great detail. However, Storin said police crime statistics were suggesting a downturn. There had been some tragic times in Boston, but things seemed to be changing for the better as crime rates began to fall.

As I soon found out, Boston had the same deeply entrenched sub-culture of gangs, guns, drugs and street feuds as all American cities. Beyond its historical past and leafy middle-class suburbs, there was a pervasive undercurrent of poverty, decaying public housing and endless street violence. I have covered only a few of the worst of these incidents during my time on the *Boston Globe* news desk.

Historic Boston

History-drenched Boston sprawls along the banks of the Charles River at the centre of a prosperous region of around 100 cities and towns forming one of the principal industrial areas in America. Boston is the scene of several key events of the American Revolution: Boston Massacre, Boston Tea Party, Battle of Bunker Hill and the Siege of Boston (see Wikipedia Boston). It had a population of 575,000 (675,000 in 2023) and together with 37 nearby communities it formed the Boston Metropolitan Area, one of the oldest municipalities in America. Puritan settlers from the English town of Boston had founded the city on the Shawmut Peninsula in 1630.

Yet it was impossible to escape the backdrop of terror and tragedy anywhere in America, even in Boston. The city had large areas of squalid housing plagued by gangs, guns, drugs, shootings and armed robberies. The annual homicide rate had worsened once again and killings were close to the 98 homicides from two years before, although the city's record was 152 homicides in 1990.

Police said the corpses dumped on street corners were again somewhat commonplace and shootings and armed robberies were daily news events. Impoverished public housing and chronic poverty seemed to drive crime along and the unpredictable violence was a constant and troubling source of crime coverage for the *Boston Globe*, one of the most famous and historic newspapers in America.

*

The *Boston Globe* newsroom was impressive by its sheer size, and the ranks of computer terminals and desks stretched away into the far distance and the football-field size newsroom was manned 24 hours a day. The *Boston Globe* had 1,850 employees in 1995 including 420 newsroom journalists, a bureau of eight in Washington and one each in New Orleans, Miami, Los Angeles, New York, Tokyo, Jerusalem, Berlin and Moscow.

However, the city had two competing newspapers, the *Boston Globe* and the *Boston Herald* and this created a state of rivalry as news teams from both papers ought to outdo the other in coverage of breaking crime and police investigations. This had the added effect of giving more visible prominence to Boston's crime environment.

Pam Shaw, Rookie Reporter

The day I arrived the crime desk sent me out with rookie night reporter Pam Shaw to seek comments from the family of a 17-year-old youth, who had been shot and killed the night before. This is referred to by newspapers as a 'death knock' and a television news crew was already driving off as we arrived in a lower-class neighbourhood. The boy's mother sobbed as she spoke to us about her son, saying how he had been interested in school and had been rebuilding a car he had bought, which sat out against the side fence. It was one more daunting yet familiar scenario for Shaw but as the late-night reporter she received a larger share of death knocks than other reporters.

Shaw told me she had worked as a reporter for less than four months after starting as a student reporter. She struggled through her first few cases while on night shift, one involving two women killed in a road accident and the driver had left the scene. Shaw managed to get an interview with the husband of one of the dead women after she told him it might help find the motorist. The man agreed, but then he cried right through the interview. Shaw said she had covered many such upsetting and tragic crime incidents in her short time on the paper. "I don't know how many murders I have covered," she said.

Gangs with Guns

The Boston Police Department had listed 10 of Boston's 63 large public housing estates as serious crime zones after they featured prominently in police crime summary reports. Assaults, robberies and drug offences were the most frequent crimes here and many homicides were never solved. Boston recorded 85 homicides in 1994. Guns were used in three of every four homicides and 67 assailants had not been identified. The police summary report showed that African Americans accounted for a disproportionate 72 per cent of the victims. Police attributed most of these killings to gangs and drugs.

The first was a shocker for me, a double murder involving a married couple in their mid-fifties, Juan and Teresa Cardon, who were stabbed to death in their home and daughter had found the bodies. Neighbours described them as a quiet, friendly couple and police had no suspects or motives.

In another incident three youths shot and killed a man during a burglary, and two more were charged with a home invasion attempt. One of the suspects was shot and wounded by police when he refused to lay down his 9-millimetre Glock semi-automatic.

Later the same week a 17-year-old youth died and a second boy was injured in two separate shootings. A neighbour called police after hearing shots and found the first youth face-down outside his house and the male caller said he appeared to be dead, "There was just some blood coming out of his mouth, but he wasn't moving." The second youth was found lying on a porch in a nearby suburb after being shot in the stomach.

Veteran Bill Doherty

Serious crime was no longer unusual in Boston according to veteran reporter Bill Doherty, who had spent 20 years covering police, courts and trials. Serious crimes like homicide no longer carried the same shock impact or were treated as seriously by editors. He said the morning's newspaper featured a report on the front of the Metro section about a student who held an imitation pistol to his teacher's head, yet the story had been placed on an inside page. There was another homicide that same morning, taking homicides, suicides, and violent deaths for the week to four.

In other shootings a girl aged eight was critically injured from a gunshot fired by an 11-year-old girl, and another girl aged 16 was murdered near the back of her high school. Doherty said these were not out of the ordinary for the *Boston Globe*.

But news interest in crime coverage had broadened somewhat to other social issues over the past 10 years. Violent crimes no longer commanded the same general interest and writing about them did not help anyone to a better life. He said there clearly was still definite interest in dramatic crime news, which was shown in the morbid fascination with the OJ Simpson trial. It had the grabbing power that made people want to read it. But readers had lost interest in routine crime, so the newspaper had to decide whether placing too many resources on crime reporting was cost-efficient. "It's trying to find a balance," he said.

Doherty said 50 per cent of the random shootings and violence in Boston involved teenagers and that made them more commonplace and more shocking, and mostly they were all strongly linked to gangs and drug violence.

The *Boston Globe* had a solid, experienced news desk with a tradition of crime coverage and a sense of pride in keeping to an established code of behaviour. He said police and newspapers had developed a mature almost symbiotic relationship and both sides worked together against crime and in the public interest. This was a throwback to the old-style police reporting from decades before when newspapers and police thought nothing of working together informally in crime reporting.

City Editor Teresa Hanafin

Teresa Hanafin said her philosophy and that of the paper was to provide coverage of crime without overdoing it by staying somewhere 'in the middle'. Hanafin said the *Boston Globe* was not like the *Los Angeles Times*, which did not cover individual homicides. Instead, the paper took a 'set back position' to do in-depth research pieces on trends. It was not easy treading the middle line because Boston did not have the same high level of violent crime as other cities, but it did have frequent homicides with 85 in 1994.

"We can't afford to ignore it, it's more of a balancing act." The paper needed to manage its resources and choose which crimes to give emphasis to:

> We do pay attention to crime here, but I'll be damned if I'm going to let murder become an acceptable crime in the city so that people become inured to it. But not to be like LA or New York, and not just tell people over and over the crimes that have been committed, but to have the responsibility to give them hope and help them with solutions and to be examining the root causes.

Court Reporting

Court reporting featured prominently in the *Boston Globe*'s crime coverage. One sensational court report published that day was about the murder of Paxton Police Chief Robert Mortell in 1994. Worcester Superior Court found a 26-year-old Boston man, Michael Souza, guilty of murder in the first degree. Mortell had been shot in the back and side when he chased two of three housebreak suspects. He was a father of three and his murder profoundly affected the two small communities where he lived and worked, and his murder was described by defence attorney Michael Hussy as a 'premeditated ambush'.

Souza received life imprisonment without the possibility of parole and his widow sobbed in the courtroom when the verdict was read out.

Another murder case that was profoundly cold-blooded involved off-duty Boston Detective John Mulligan, who had been working on a paid security detail outside Walgreen's Drug Store in Roslindale on September 26, 1993. Mulligan had been asleep in his Ford Explorer when he was shot five times in the face with a small calibre handgun. There was $147 still in his pocket when the body was discovered.

The prosecution alleged that the two defendants before the court had shot Mulligan then reached in and taken his 9-millimetre Glock service pistol to keep as a trophy. It was unclear which of the two accused had pulled the trigger, Sean Ellis, then 19, or his accomplice, Terry Patterson. However, successive re-trials (Ellis had four) saw Patterson released from jail in 2006 and Ellis in 2016. The prosecution said it did not intend to re-charge either of the defendants.

John Ellement was the court reporter but before that he had been police reporter for four years and he understood many of the underlying demands, complexities, pitfalls and techniques of providing coverage of crime and police. One point he made was how important it was to do your own leg work.

Ellement said he pulled court records whenever he was examining individual cases, and this gave him names, dates, criminal records, addresses, friends, girlfriends and family members. He did not expect or get a lot of direct help from the police. Often, he arrived at a crucial street address before the police got there which usually infuriated them. He took pride in this as it set him apart and made his stories fresher and different.

Gun Running

State Attorney Donald Stern called a press conference after arrests were made over a gun-running operation from Jackson, Mississippi. Stern displayed a table laid out with 15 firearms including a TEC-22, Mac-11 and a 12-gauge shotgun. I was invited to attend to see the weapons for myself. It reminded me of the car boot sale for guns I had seen in Atlanta where in a festival environment people gathered to buy and sell guns from collections in cars. No gun licenses were needed to buy or sell guns in Georgia.

Stern said one offender, Jose Andrade, 21, served as an example of how guns were being brought into the city. Andrade had been arrested for buying automatic pistols and assault weapons in Mississippi where guns were easily and cheaply obtained. He drove them back into Boston where they were sold to his friends and used to commit various criminal offences. Stern said Andrade had picked up the weapons at pawn shops and gun shows and then drove them across state lines where he sold them at a massive profit. Gun laws were more lenient in

Mississippi where the only statute regulating gun sales made it unlawful to put a deadly weapon in the hands of a minor or someone who was intoxicated.

The seizure of Andrade's guns had helped to reduce violent crime in Upham's Corner, where there had been 22 shootings in the first three months of 1995 compared with 90 in the first three months of the year before.

Newspapers Distorting Crime

Supt. James M. Claiborne said newspapers presented crime, violence and disorder more frequently and graphically in Boston. In part, this reflected competition between two strong crime-reporting newspapers, the *Boston Globe* and the *Boston Herald*. This rivalry between news agencies led to more urgent coverage of violent crime, creating an impression that violence was getting worse when it was not.

He sometimes got upset over newspaper reports but he understood that news was a competitive business and a product to be sold. But where a mistake was made police could present their side. "There has been a great deal of fear generated. But we are a very open organisation. If we make a mistake then we accept responsibility." He said a case a year before, where a SWAT team raided the wrong home and a church minister died of a heart attack, had put police 'unfavourably' in the public eye, but the police were given the chance to put their side. Admitting a mistake was important in cases where police were at fault.

Supt. Claiborne said a watchdog group had found that newspapers devoted three times more space to crime than any other issue. More attention was given to violent crime, which was more graphic and more widely shown. Newspapers could take a closer role in covering crime or as educators as a mechanism to help find solutions to Boston's violent crime problems, "But is anyone interested in that? It would be interesting to see how much people read in other sections of the paper."

Newspaper reporters had learned their craft in the 'laboratory of the streets' and in time this led to more balanced accounts of crime and police affairs as reporters became more experienced. Crime and police reporters used formal and informal channels for their information, but they relied chiefly on a personal network of mostly unidentified police officers for tip-offs and background colour. Many young police officers did not understand the role of the press or the way reporters treated issues. But generally, there was a balanced response to crime reporting but newspapers also gave an editorial position as part of their role.

He said Boston's violent crime was equal to 20 years before but the big difference was the guns. There was also clear evidence that victims and offenders were younger every year. Boston's annual homicide rate was 97 averaged over 20 years but in 1994 it had fallen to 85 from 98 the year before. Crime rates had fallen progressively since 1975 when the department recorded 80,530 reported crimes. By 1994 the number had fallen to 53,078, burglaries from 18,892 to 6,799, robberies from 7,778 to 4,245 and vehicle theft from 28,219 to 11,240. But rates for violent crimes like homicide and rape were unchanged. Crime rates had fallen also for crimes like rape but he said an emphasis on crime by newspapers had distorted the reality.

The police department had 'torn down the wall' that used to exist and had won support from experts and most areas of the community. Community policing was heralded as a return to the 1930s when police walked a beat and got to know the locals and neighbourhoods instead of being 'driven by the 911 system'.

A lot of players were taking responsibility for the community and 700 Crime Watch programs had been set up to meet a variety of problems. Police regularly visited Boston's comprehensive educational institutions, which were unpaid consultants and gave police top-level advice and examined new police proposals.

Boston was improving its public housing by introducing individual entrances and creating a better green and personal space. "It stops treating people like cattle and that has worked." People were taking more pride in their properties and Supt. Claiborne said it was helping to develop a sense of community, and many housing projects were being turned into cooperatives.

Boston Police did not suffer from corruption though, mainly because Boston was not a corrupt city. "We're not at all a brutal department," he said. Police had not killed anyone in the line of duty for three years and only averaged about 10 firearm discharges a year. However, police were seizing about 1,500 guns a year.

Boston had reached its highest annual death toll in 1990 with 152 homicides, so police formed an anti-gang unit, and this had met with striking success by reducing homicides and violent crime. But Supt. Claiborne said he was 'quietly proud' of his department's ability to peg back Boston's crime rate, especially homicides. Boston was a vibrant city where people could walk the streets at night and where high crime areas were not desolate like other cities. "It's going very, very well here," he said.

Falling Circulation

Average weekday circulation for the Boston Globe was 505,000 and 815,265 on Sundays. Its main local competition, the *Boston Herald*, had a weekday circulation of 300,000 and 215,000 on Sundays. Like the *Boston Globe* the *Herald* gave a strong focus on crime and law enforcement and this rivalry was generating heightened interest and efforts to be the first with breaking news.

By the start of 2018 the *Boston Globe's* weekday circulation had fallen from 505,000 to 120,876. Sunday circulation was down from 815,265 to 213,206 (Problems Piling Up at the Boston Globe – Layoffs, Falling Circulation, and Multiple Investigations, *GoLocalProv.com*, May 2018).

The *Boston Globe* was founded in 1873 by the Taylor family which owned the newspaper until 1993 when it was bought by the *New York Times*. William Taylor was still running the newspaper in 1995.

Chapter 7
Toronto, Canada

Gangs Battle over Drugs

Canada was struggling against an inbound flood of crack cocaine which began arriving soon after 1986 dislodging heroin as the drug of choice. The rise of cocaine sparked furious street battles as drug dealers fought for control of the lucrative drugs trade.

Toronto had also faced the rise of an Asian gang war in 1991 when Chinese Triads gained a foothold in Canada. *The Toronto Star* recorded the rising climate of urban violence stemming from ethnic Vietnamese street gangs, which were also carrying out home invasions and running credit card scams. Cocaine had only recently become a focus for this new wave of violence, mainly in the less affluent public housing estates where poor blacks, whites and Asians lived alongside each other.

Gangs and drugs were also causing serious problems for society and for police and the courts in Canada. But they were on a completely different scale to America. Toronto had just hit a record 87 murders in 1994 for a population of 4.3 million and there were 596 homicides for all of Canada with a population of 29.3 million. By comparison, the city of Chicago had 930 homicides the same year with a population of 2.7 million. Few other cities or countries had anything resembling the relentless, dysfunctional crime environment as American cities. Nor did Canada have anything on the scale of the massive decaying public housing estates or street gangs as Chicago or Los Angeles.

Crime coverage by *The Toronto Star* was not driven by the same intensity of round-the-clock shootings and homicides as its near neighbour. However, *The Toronto Star* based crime coverage on America's crime reporting formula, although there was a noticeable coldness in the air concerning relations with police in Canada. And a bitterly contested war of words over controversial cases was playing out in the courts between *The Toronto Star* and the Metro Toronto Police.

The Toronto Star crime desk was determined to provide its readers with comprehensive crime and police coverage. Reporters manned a dedicated 'police room' with seven police scanners listening in to the Metro Toronto Police, regional and provincial police agencies and fire and ambulance services. They called Metro Toronto Police every hour, but this was not really closeness. *The Toronto Star* and police were more like bitter adversaries in the public space, which exploded regularly with bitter accusations and counteraccusations, a very public animosity.

In 1995, Toronto had a population of more than 6 million and a substantial police presence. The Toronto Police had around 5,500 uniformed officers for the greater metropolitan area and the Ontario Provincial Police had another 4,000 to handle crime along the highways or in smaller communities. The Royal Canadian Mounted Police concerned itself with federal offences and was a cousin to America's Federal Bureau of Investigation.

City Editor Dave Ellis

Dave Ellis said *The Toronto Star* was challenging the limits placed on publishing by the courts and the police. The courts had ruled that the right to a fair trial did not always outweigh the rights of the press to publish its own research. This concept had not yet been tested in the courts and Ellis was waiting for that opportunity to come along.

Reporters were prepared to bypass police and develop other sources. "We don't have a crime rate here that cities in the states have," Ellis said. "So, we put time and resources into covering stories in depth by going to other sources not just police."

Examples of stories the paper had produced during the year ranged from straight reporting to feature-length articles based on analysis, opinion and research. *The Toronto Star* was examining evidence a police officer was corrupt and ways to prepare a report about it. It involved a black drug pusher who had shot and killed a police officer during raid and police had returned fire wounding him. It later came to light that the police were involved in a series of drug plants on known drug dealer suspects. A reporter was assigned to prepare a dossier on the suspect and the police involved to find out everything he could. "That's going to be one hell of a story," Ellis said.

In another case Ellis sent a young reporter to work undercover at a school for 10 months posing as a student. The result was a blow-by-blow exposé on school life. Ellis said he did not understand regular education reporting, so he decided it needed to be told by the students themselves.

The paper was taking a broader road to crime reporting, seeking richer inside stories of crime and police. Reporters would use official police channels but would find ways to get behind the police to deliver a fully independent version of events. These methods were producing highly original crime stories that read more like entertainment and were based on unusual perspectives, a very different style of crime coverage built around the deep involvement of the reporters themselves.

This questions where the boundaries should be for newspapers. Should they be constrained by official authorities, the justice system, courts and police? Or was their duty as journalists just to report events as they were presented to them, usually echoing the line prepared by professional PR managers working for corporations, police departments and government agencies?

One argument in favour of this approach was the way it enabled *The Toronto Star* reporters to expose the underside of the systemic nature of society. It was unlikely traditional reporting methods would have penetrated or upset the official status quo.

Pushing the Boundaries

Nick Pron and John Duncanson (who passed in 2009, age 43) were investigative journalists covering police and crime, working as a team on special investigative projects. Pron had been on the police beat for 20 years and Duncanson for six. They said they held police in low esteem but still dealt with them wherever they could to build contacts and keep in touch with developments. This included going to favoured police watering holes, where they spent time getting to know what police were saying and working on.

The Toronto Star was pushing the boundaries beyond straight news reporting and Pron and Duncanson were almost invasive in their aggressive style. This must have had a decisive impact on confidence in Metro Toronto Police operations because neither of them called the police media over issues they were reporting on. Instead, they relied on their own police contacts at sergeant rank and above and they often interviewed witnesses before the police did. Duncanson had twice appeared as a witness for the prosecution in homicide trials. They looked for trends or submerged themselves in particularly complex cases, priding themselves on staying a few steps ahead of police investigations. It was almost as if they were police themselves.

"I get really involved with murders and in the first few days I go head-to-head with the cops," Duncanson said. "We interview suspects even before the police get to them." The two reporters concentrated on unsolved crimes or they examined gang profiles. Toronto also had its own large dysfunctional public housing estates, and the two reporters gave their perspectives. "Everything is destroyed," Duncanson said. "There are no trees or grass, only rows and rows of tenement housing. It's scary to go in there."

Pron and Duncanson were working on one of the biggest and most controversial of Toronto's recent crimes, a murder/rape case involving businessman Paul Kenneth Bernardo, who had been charged with the rape and murder of three teenage girls. He faced a further 17 rape charges and his wife, Karla Homolka, was already behind bars over two of the murders. She had agreed to be the chief witness for the prosecution against Bernardo.

Pron and Duncanson had spent three years carrying out research for a special four-page feature to be published after the trial. *The Toronto Star* routinely observed sub judice restrictions on publishing once an arrest was made. But it was making an exception in this case and had already published numerous researched articles.

Bernardo was convicted of several offences in 1995, including two first-degree murders and two aggravated sexual assaults and he was sentenced to life in prison without parole for at least 25 years. He was designated a dangerous offender making him unlikely to be released.

'Testi-lying'

A lengthy weekend article on *The Toronto Star*'s front page accused police of 'testi-lying' over the suspension and charging of four Metro Toronto Police for planting drugs on suspects. The headline read: 'True lies: More and more the word of the police is questioned':

A cloud hangs over Metro Police 12 Division, where four officers from the same platoon have been suspended and charged with fabricating evidence and obstructing justice in a narcotics case. In the United States, allegations of police dishonesty have been well documented. It even has a nickname: Testi-lying. Why would police act dishonestly? Some legal experts feel it's the inevitable by-product of legal rules set up to exclude evidence if it's obtained in violation of a suspect's rights.

Defence lawyer Peter Zaduk was reported saying, "I think I'd go so far as to say that after 17 years of practising there is not another category of witness that resorts to falsehoods more often than the police." It was not a healthy indicator of a fruitful police-newspaper relationship.

Falling Circulation

The Toronto Star was the biggest newspaper in Canada and one of three major metropolitan mastheads in Toronto, the others being *The Globe and Mail* and *Toronto Sun*. It had a massive newsroom with around 350-editorial staff of a total workforce of 1,500. Daily circulation averaged 500,000 and 800,000 on Saturdays, on the same scale as the *Boston Globe*. It ranked as one of the most influential newspapers in North America. But by 2019 weekday circulation had plunged to 193,050 on average and 290,153 on Saturdays (The Toronto Star Media Kit, 2019).

Chapter 8
Manchester, England

The criminal justice system in England and Scotland was a difficult environment for newspapers to penetrate. All they wanted was enough details about emerging crimes to be able to report them with some clarity, understanding, depth, colour and meaning. But this was something they never seemed to achieve. Violence was commonplace in the large slum neighbourhoods in cities like Manchester, where stand-over tactics and muscle were used to enforce the local drugs trade. But newspaper relations with the police were marked by officiousness, formality and a general suppression of information about police investigations.

It was a stunning contrast with America, where diligent reporters had forged enduring ties with unnamed operational police and where news coverage was still rich in detail and colour. A failure of British police to develop ways of informing newspapers had progressively broken down any chance of working together in covering crime. Newspapers had a vested interest in obtaining details of crimes from primary sources like the police, but crime stories needed sufficient detail to qualify as a page lead or even as the newspaper's lead story. TV needed far less to include a crime story in the news, but TV news usually had very little context or explanation anyway.

Police indifference towards newspapers had been evident in Canada as well as Australia through my own direct experiences. In Britain, newspapers had gradually cut back on crime coverage over the years and had come to rely on police media releases, which were usually rewritten into briefs. More detailed coverage was left to court reporters during subsequent coverage of trials usually months later. Few newspapers could get context, relevance, background and colour for breaking crime incidents and this standoff seemed permanent and everywhere. Many reporters said it was frustrating to be denied access to sufficient details to be able to explain incidents to readers. Not surprisingly they blamed the police.

Biggest Crime Story of the Year

The *Manchester Evening News* rushed headlong towards its final afternoon deadline, while tens of thousands of office and factory workers were getting ready to pour from the commercial centre out to the suburbs by bus and train. A few minutes before 6 pm the pace begins to slacken and the news desk empties as the last page is being read through to be sent to the printers. The early editions were already on the streets for commuters to read on the way home as they streamed out from the business centre.

Editor Michael Unger hunched forward as he peered into a computer terminal in the dim moving shadows of the newsroom, his shirtsleeves were rolled up as he worked shoulder-to-shoulder with his news editor, reporters and sub-editors. Everyone had a part to play in this purposeful scene. The mood was one of intimacy and cheerful teamwork and no one said anything not related to the task at hand.

Eyes kept lifting to the clock on the wall and I noticed beads of sweat on Unger's brow as he looked up to nod hello. The *Manchester Evening News* was putting the finishing touches to its 6 pm edition, the final print run for a total of five separate editions that day written for four geographic distribution zones.

Unger was very much a hands-on editor of the old school. He personally designed the front page each day and stayed involved with all processes of news production. Now he was working on a newly updated lead story for the final edition. Not too far from the editor, several teenage copy kids sat around on a wooden beam wearing identifying white shirts, ready to dart off to deliver messages and copy around the building.

The latest draft of a national crime news story had just landed on Unger's desk from police reporter Steve Panter, who was on assignment in Liverpool. Unger was reading it and sketching out how the front page would be shaped. Panter's story was leading the paper today about the controversial appearance in the witness box of former Manchester Police Chief, John Stalker (passed 2019). Stalker was an important witness in a civil court action by British millionaire Kevin Taylor, who was claiming malicious prosecution and conspiracy. The affair related to the time Stalker held an inquiry into the alleged 'shoot to kill' policy, which was linked to the death of suspected members of the Provisional Irish Republican Army in 1982.

An 'embarrassed' British Government was trying to prevent Stalker appearing in the witness box. Panter reported that the case was 'sensationally halted on the grounds of national security. The headline Unger places on the story reads: "Govt bid to gag Stalker, Taylor cash fight delay." It was the paper's biggest crime story of the year.

The front page was finally given the all-clear and Unger and the old hands, cadets, reporters and news editors trooped out of the newsroom, leaving it to the silence and shadows until early the next morning, when they would come back and do it all again.

*

Greater Manchester is Britain's second city of more than three million people with around 800,000 in the metropolitan area, which features large areas of run-down housing, industrial estates and tens of thousands of families living in squalid cityscapes. The conurbation swallowed up the cities of Manchester and Salford, the towns of Bolton, Bury, Oldham, Rochdale, Stockport and Wigan and the boroughs of Tameside and Trafford.

Britain was a visibly stratified society in 1995 with extremes of rich, middle-class and poor and with large urban areas dominated by a sprawling working underclass. Income and wealth were expressed in lifestyle, dress, spoken language and demography, and the social structure was visibly defined in Manchester with its distinctive urban pockets of squalor near and around industrial zones.

The decision-makers, politicians, corporate elites and sporting celebrities who featured regularly in the news did not live near urban backwaters like Moss Side-Hume, which was essentially the province of street gangs. They belonged to the middle- and upper-income brackets, living mainly in tree-lined estates or in lavish country manors scattered around the countryside, notably in nearby Cheshire, home to many of Manchester United's footballing families. These same social elites dominated the news and expected to have their own views and morality reproduced in newspapers.

Manchester Evening News

Newspapers like the *Manchester Evening News* operated in a climate that was strongly biased against mounting any crime crusades, and crime coverage suffered somewhat from the notoriously ultra-conservative British police establishment. Reporters were forced to negotiate with highly rigid authoritarian police forces and their formalised avenues of information. This had a deadening effect on the production of news and the concept of crime as newsworthy subject matter. There were also strict legal constraints from the courts and criminal justice system, which were strongly weighted against publishing crime news for fear of spoiling a fair trial.

The *Manchester Evening News* headquarters at 164 Deansgate was in the heart of Manchester, home of Old Trafford and the Manchester United Football Club. The layout was divided into curious rabbit warrens featuring old oak doors and polished tiles, with that aged feel of mulled wine in old oak casks, and there was a sense of dust and tradition in the air. The paper had been founded in 1869 as an election sheet before being bought by the *Manchester Guardian*, itself formed about 1820. It was now a tabloid, but it was a conservative paper that did not exploit muckraking or sensationalise sex, crime or trivia the way the British tabloid press is supposed to do. It certainly did not overdo or exploit crime and police reporting. The paper prided itself on a responsible and conservative approach to its news coverage and it took a moderate line with crime news.

The paper's basic philosophy was to take a cautious approach to crime and the police culture. These issues were not as essentially newsworthy or important to a big-city newspaper concerned by appearance, dignity and market rating, politics and the economy. But the paper led by Michael Unger aimed to write for its readers' tastes and therefore the issues raised did have a tabloid feel or presentation. In this way, the *Manchester Evening News* stood apart from Britain's more conservative broadsheets.

In general terms the paper reflected the same crime gathering techniques as newspapers in all western democracies. It did not seek to explore or explain Manchester's chronic crime problems or venture too much into the run-down estates. The paper, reflecting its industry, was unlikely to inquire in any consistent way into the plight of prison inmates, conditions in jails or the environments and lifestyles that drive crime.

But times were already changing and the *Manchester Evening News* was about to bring down the curtain on this quaint era, with the imminent changeover to computerised typesetting and page design. It would end the days of typed news copy and pages pasted together in mosaics by printing compositors. But it was unlikely to change the tradition of news production linked to people like Michael Unger.

Greater Manchester Police

Manchester's rate of burglary detection was the worst in Britain. The Metropolitan Police said figures suggested that 95 per cent of all burglaries and robberies across the UK were not being solved (The Guardian, 2018). Police were swamped with crime and searching for new strategies to deal with them.

But the 7,000 strong Greater Manchester Police was under a cloud as well. It was one of seven large police forces in Britain that had stopped automatically attending emergency calls, saying up to a third of all crime reports were just too expensive to deal with and were handled over the telephone. Police in Manchester were accused of being too slow to respond to many of the 416,873 emergency 999 calls in 1994 – as a result, 2,653 complaints were lodged.

Murder was a rare event in Manchester though with only around 30 to 40 a year. This infrequency should make them news events. The *Manchester Evening News* did not put them on page 1 or dress them up with banner headlines for inside pages. It appeared to be a sentiment linked more to broken-down relations with unhelpful police and a lack of interest in covering routine crime events, including car thefts, burglaries and drug busts. Inner-city crime zones like Moss Side-Hume had chronic poverty, sub-standard housing, drugs and gangs, all of which gave police a constant headache. But this did not translate into newspaper interest.

Cannabis and heroin were the dominant illegal drugs in Manchester in the mid- to late-1990s, which police felt they could deal with. A climate of rising drug imports of crack cocaine, however, had provoked gang turf wars in Salford and Cheetham Hill. But these abated when unofficial treaties, which police helped to write, were struck by warring gangs. After that, killings and gang battles declined somewhat, and gangs stayed inside their own territorial boundaries. For a time at least, all sides recognised each other's right to a place in the scheme of things.

Police reserved the right of entry to the streets, and they deliberately kept up patrols to the worst areas. They would not allow exclusion zones and made sure they carried out regular foot patrols. "We are there to enforce our right to be there," a senior police officer told me. "You can't do it out of vans with helmets."

Nor was Britain a gun-focused society and it was unusual for firearms to be used in crime. Firearms were not kept in private homes except as an exception to the rule and controlled by strict licensing conditions. Gun licences were difficult to obtain except by bona fide shooting enthusiasts or farmers. Police generally did not carry side-arms either. But guns were becoming a greater menace in Britain in 1995, which police told me they were increasingly worried about. Crimes usually involved theft and loss of property rather than violence such as domestic or gang disputes in cities like Manchester. This type of violence was not well reported anywhere anyway and certainly not by the *Manchester Evening News*.

Boundaries of Trust

Detective Chief Inspector Bill Noble, from Manchester's Crime Investigation Support Division, gave me a police perspective on the patchy interface between police operations and newspapers. He said there were two or three levels of newspaper police reporting. The first was the crudest, where reporters called to stations each day for the latest details of routine crime, which were generally used as fillers.

Then there were more experienced reporters, who covered unusual or bigger crimes and who developed closer relations with operational police. Ideally, this relationship should help police to obtain good press or sympathy. Reporters needed the ability to obtain access to the police to write solid coverage of crime news and police events.

Inspector Noble said relations between police and reporters were 'mutual' with benefits accruing to either side. Some stories had the potential to be critical of police, and in those circumstances police tended to be more guarded in what they said. "This is where the trust level comes in, where you give [only] background to them," he said.

Police were always touchy about criticism, Inspector Noble said. Some spoke frankly and openly to a reporter then sat back to see how it was reported. Under these circumstances police were prepared to speak out just to see where the ripples went. Police held media conferences for major crimes, which were structured and calculated to get the best return of information for investigations.

Most police followed the rules, but Inspector Noble said few if any would be prepared to lie or rebut a truth. "That is the system we operate by."

Reporters often agreed to provide police with a draft copy of a feature story before it ran. This was not so much for police to make changes but to be forewarned about the content of the story, enabling police to have a game plan ready when the phone started ringing the next day.

Inspector Noble gave a pencil sketch of crime in Manchester. Auto theft accounted for 30 per cent of all offences, which was a low-risk crime, whereas burglary entailed higher risks. In turn, burglaries were driven largely by illegal drugs. Police did not take a rigid stance over lesser drug offences like marijuana and handed out cautions for small amounts. He said it would be pointless to prosecute them, but police pursued major drug traffickers with great determination.

Greater Manchester Police was the second-biggest police force in Britain, behind the London Metropolitan Police, which had 27,700 sworn officers. The Manchester Police was the third-largest force per capita of the 42 police forces in England and Wales, which had overall manpower of 125,813 officers in 1994.

Changing the Police Culture

Digging out information from police was just as hard for the Greater Manchester Police Press Office at Chester House. The civilian media managers, Richard Flynn and Mary Todd, said police trusted them less than they trusted reporters. "It goes all through the force from top to bottom," Flynn said. "Police are bad at taking advice from somebody else."

Police in Manchester and in Britain more generally were not media friendly. They routinely refused to give out information even to their own press office. But at least police media was generally better being managed by civilian professionals like themselves rather than by the police. Sometimes they were made to look foolish when they could not answer questions from the media. Their standard reply was, "We have no crystal ball." But the flow of information was better than it used to be, and the press office answered all questions put to them unless there were strong reasons not to.

Flynn said newspapers were responsible for upholding laws governing publication not the police. Generally speaking, newspapers felt that the editor was the best judge of what should go in the paper then he or she alone would wear the consequences of any decisions. Police have trouble with this concept.

Perhaps it comes down to keeping control of situations as police traditionally seek to do as a right in the course of their operations. This was a touchy issue but an important one for police-media relations. Sub judice came into effect from the time of arrest and this was controlled under the *Contempt of Court Act*. Charge details can be released but not the names of those who have been arrested.

Flynn and Todd said their aim was to help the media not to block questions. "Ultimately we have a moral duty to tell journalists what he's doing could be contempt of court," Flynn said. He said media awareness was part of police recruitment training but many young police were then forewarned by long-serving officers not to talk to the media, so they had to be retrained. "The only advice they ever have is 'don't say anything, I've heard rumours they are dangerous so don't tell them anything'." Flynn had recently given a police seminar about his role as a facilitator, negotiator and adviser to police as well as the media. "Attempting to ensure these headlines are always favourable is the daunting aspect of the job."

Yet the press office was always on the lookout for good news stories that showed the force in a good light. News headlines on police misbehaviour got prominence because these events were rare 'and therefore more newsworthy'. The office also dealt with prejudice from the media. Some news teams arrived with the fixed idea that all police were bad and then staff must move heaven and earth to change their attitudes. Flynn said, "I think it is a question of changing the culture."

They were wary of a rise in police reporting by freelancers who could cause headaches by taking a shallow approach to police journalism. After that they could not be trusted and it undermined ties with regular reporters. The press office wanted to give input to stories but expected a reasonable outcome for police in return.

The cost of providing technical advice to television police dramas and documentaries posed a significant drain on police resources. TV production companies were streaming into police media offices across Britain seeking help with police dramas and their workload included briefing TV script writers. In 1994 the press office assisted with productions of *The Bill, Cracker, Prime Suspect, Coronation Street* and *Brookside*.

The media office was substantial by comparison with media offices in America with21 staff and operating 14 hours a day, from 7.30 am to 10 pm in the week with a senior officer on call outside those hours.

Falling Circulation

The *Manchester Evening News* was Britain's biggest evening newspaper with a circulation of 220,000 for a readership of 650,000. It also produced Britain's biggest free weekly newspaper, the *Metro News,* with 324,000 copies all distributed on Fridays. Its closest rival in 1995 was the *Daily Mirror*, which then sold 187,000 copies each weekday. By 2018 circulation for the *Manchester Evening News* had collapsed from 220,000 to 36,715.

Chapter 9
Edinburgh, Scotland

The Scotsman

Marcello Mega had won the Scottish Reporter of the Year award for his investigations into the infamous Robert Black affair (working with fellow reporter Alan Hutchison), involving the murder of three schoolgirls in the 1980s (Britain's Most Prolific Child Killer, *Daily Mail*, January 2016).

Mega told me he was in touch with police almost every day but he was wary of their motives because "what they tell you is what they want you to know." Police would help him with details of minor crimes like muggings and they would cooperate with information about more serious crimes. But they refused to provide many of the details, sometimes as trivial as the value of stolen goods or the amount of cash taken in a robbery. They would give broader background, such as whether suspects were being sought, but only when this might help their investigations by persuading a witness to come forward.

It was essential for the newspaper to publish full coverage of crime including the value of robberies or the amount of cash stolen. The patchy quality of police information often left him unable to put together a decent story. On the other hand, police were very helpful with murder cases although they tended to release information in 'dribs and drabs'. They would use the media to test whether each release of information advanced their investigations.

Mega said winning trust was the overwhelming secret and police reporting was far more productive when he was able to work one-on-one with individual police. He sought access to senior police to discuss cases, provide background and fill in the gaps without quoting them in stories. But usually these police had an agenda of their own, to open information channels or dig up evidence. Winning over high-level contacts did not come easily either. It took him four years of hard work before he managed to get a senior officer willing to talk with him 'off the record'. Until then he had been stuck with 'the official line'.

He recently obtained access to another senior police contact and this was making a big difference to his output and the quality of his crime coverage. It also meant he was better placed to know what he should and should not say in the newspaper about sensitive cases. Mega said it was more convenient for police to refer reporters to the police press office, which kept reporters out of the hair of operational police. But it had the effect of reducing the quality of contact instead of improving it. The press office in Edinburgh told me later that they were having problems with reporters from *The Scotsman*.

In one example of this breakdown in communications, a police office in Edinburgh had been burgled three years before and many confidential files stolen, including the identities of undercover officers and police informants. This was a serious blow to police, but they refused to admit the extent of the loss and continued to say that little of importance was missing. It was an example of why police and the media should be prepared to work together. The missing files were later handed to reporter Alan Hutchinson which revealed just what had been taken. The newspaper ran some controversial stories on the matter but police were angry about publishing their files and relations were soured for a long time.

Reporter Severan Carrell

Severan Carrell handled much of the politics of police and larger or longer-running issues, such as Scottish nationalist terrorism. He had broken a big Scottish story about the discovery of an Irish Republican Army cell in 1993, which he followed right to the Old Bailey in London.

His most recent report was about police bugging, which he found had increased significantly over the previous year. The Lothian and Borders Police refused to respond to his requests for comment, saying the issue was too obscure and of no real value to the public. Carrell said police were unwilling to debate such issues because they wanted to control what went to the media. They had issued a two-line press release immediately before his story went to press. Such releases by police are regarded by reporters as a dirty trick because they spoil the sense of exclusivity. This happened frequently when reporters sought inside information on unpopular police issues or operations as a form of pay-back.

Carrell said most police and crime stories were handled by reporters on the spot in regional offices or by London or Glasgow bureaus. This is where

Scotland's biggest crime stories emerged, where there were far higher levels of property or violent crime than in Edinburgh. He said the police media had improved its information on crime and sent out press notices through a wire service. But Carrell noted that the newspaper's handling of police calls had deteriorated from two years before, when duty reporters would call police, fire and ambulance each hour.

Editor James Seaton

James Seaton said that since the newspaper already supported law and order they would not be too far out of line with police. "If we step on a few toes that is too bad," he said. "We believe in law and order so we would inevitably be on the same side as police. But we have a duty as a newspaper to ensure police are doing their job properly and being above board and straight."

Seaton said *The Scotsman* monitored allegations of police corruption even-handedly and he made sure that claims of racism or domestic violence were treated properly. A newspaper must be able to stand back and look harshly at all issues, not only at police but health services, politicians and any other public or private body. "We are all the public has to protect them from abuses by police." Seaton said relations with the police were tenuous, and as soon as they were criticised they stopped speaking to the media and 'the shutters would come down'. But he was also conscious of being too close to the police point of view. "The trouble with police reporters is that they are like football writers; they are too close and turn a blind eye. This is fatal for newspapers."

Having well-developed police contacts usually paid dividends when big stories came along. They also gave some common ground on issues like police corruption or mistakes and led to more willingness to see each other's point of view. But they imposed a duty of responsibility on the reporter that could amount to a conflict of interest. Without realising it a reporter could lose his independence just to get along with his police contacts. Seaton might fear a reporter turning a blind eye, but it seemed even less profitable to have no relations at all.

Crime Reporter Peter Laing

The *Edinburgh Evening News* was an afternoon paper, and it was seeking better crime news coverage to reflect its different audience, mainly commuters. *The Scotsman* was a morning paper and it tended to cover the same crime issues the *Edinburgh Evening News* had already reported the story the night before, but with an element of old news about it. This created a rivalry between reporters from both papers for access to police. But the police media relations office told me it preferred to deal with the more conservative-minded reporters from *The Scotsman*.

Laing said he wanted to cover crime news but he was getting a stony response from the police media relations office. His relationship with the police was made unnecessarily difficult because of a prevailing police culture where they were suspicious of journalists. The official line was to hand out press releases and to insist that all access was made through the police media relations office but getting constables or sergeants to talk to him was near impossible. Laing said there was a misplaced fear and worry about reporters talking to police directly and a desire for information to be controlled by the media relations office alone.

Laing had been working on the *Edinburgh Evening News* for three years and on the police beat for about a year. He went to a lot of trouble to get to know senior police and to meet specialist squads to build relations, get quotes or develop stories. He now had a small group of officers he was comfortable phoning and now he was often able to bypass the media relations office. He said the media office was not proactive on major crimes and would only give him information that was bland or would soon become general knowledge.

Laing said homicides almost always made the front page in Edinburgh, but they were comparatively rare and that left him with plenty of leg work to keep up a decent rate of other crime news.

Crimes and Offences for Edinburgh 1993–1994

Crimes	1994		1993	
	Recorded	Solved	Recorded	Solved
Homicide	13	13	13	13
Assault	927	598	841	537
Robbery	834	230	841	258
Rape	88	74	65	51
Burglary	8,320	1,577	9,253	1,733
Vehicle theft	5,476	1,628	5,438	1,371
Drugs	2,870	2,868	4,158	4,158
Firearms	121	119		

* Source: Lothian and Borders Police, Report of the Chief Constable, 1994.

Laing said he believed more information should be made freely available to the media and the journalist and newspaper editors should choose which stories to run or seek more background on. His job would be far easier if he had direct access to relevant police when required. "When there is a murder help is often non-existent and police would say 'You are just the press, and you will print what we tell you.'" That was the prevailing attitude for most police – but others were very helpful, and some even allowed him to call them at home to talk on any issue.

There was one detective superintendent Laing could ring at any time to get background information on homicides or major crimes. "It comes right down to the people they are and the personalities. It plays on any police reporter's mind what happens when you run that story that knocks police? You have got to have some ethics."

* Peter Laing was appointed news editor of *Scotland on Sunday* in 2001.
He became chief reporter for Scottish news agency *Deadline* in 2010.

Police Media

Dan Hewitt, who was a former reporter for *The Scotsman*, said it took a "more responsible" approach to covering crime, while the *Edinburgh Evening News* was prepared to run sensationalised versions of stories. Police wanted and needed feedback from the media but found they were often let down and challenged by the evening paper. The biggest concerns involved detail not always essential to the overall story, which could have been removed.

Hewitt said relations came down to common sense. If journalists were friendly and reliable they were more likely to get help. But on numerous occasions, police who spoke to *Edinburgh Evening News* reporters found their 'off the record' comments appearing in print. He said that with closer relations he was able to 'do a deal' to leave certain things out of a story in exchange for a fuller briefing or with background 'not to be quoted'. "If they go behind my back, I am not comfortable with giving guidance," Hewitt said. "You become very wary with what you are going to say."

On one occasion a journalist had rung the Chief Constable to lodge a complaint then Hewitt had been required to provide an explanation. He said that if journalists were trustworthy and responsible, he was willing to set up interviews and give them access to police. Otherwise, he was careful to say nothing unofficially. Police would give basic information but not the extra guidance to people they were uncomfortable with. "The better way of getting information out of us is by taking the other approach."

Hewitt was always surprised to find that journalists suspected there was more going on than they knew about. Some specialist police like the drug squad were expected to be doing some sort of operations. But by and large not a lot was going on that reporters did not already know about. Some relations with the media became soured because individual police were afraid of talking to civilians or journalists. Most were okay but junior police were often overcautious.

The Lothian and Borders Police had a general order explaining how to liaise with the media. It urged prompt and courteous dealings with the media but also warned of the *Contempt of Court Act*, which was applied more vigorously in Scotland than the rest of Britain. Hewitt said Scottish laws were different from those elsewhere in Britain and they used specific terminology. The two main courts were the 'Sheriff's Court' for property or violent crime (and conducted by a full-time lawyer) and the 'Court of Sessions' for higher levels of major crime.

Police were caught up in the middle of difficult restrictions on the release of information imposed by the justice system. The *Contempt of Court Act* was extremely serious if breached by police giving out unauthorised information. Elements of each police investigation were also the responsibility of the Crown Office. An example of this double handling was the issuing of police identikits (photofits), which had to be approved by the Crown Office before they could be released. Delays in seeking and getting approval for identikits often impeded the flow of information to the media and this led to animosity.

Once a writ was issued only the most basic information could be released and Scottish judges strictly enforced this law. Reporters did not understand how this red tape held up the release of information and it led to a lot of misunderstandings. To make the point about the severity of publication laws the *Daily Express* had been fined £25,000 two years before for linking the identity of an assailant with his victim.

There were other differences in the law as distinct from England and Wales which shared a common system. In Scotland two witnesses were needed for identification in court instead of one and pictures of known criminals could not be released before a trial and courts could impose strong sanctions. Charges read out in a Scottish court were worded differently to those elsewhere in Britain. The wording of the charge related directly to the circumstances of the crime and could continue for pages and this made it difficult for the press office to describe each offence when reporters asked them.

Newspapers in Scotland

The dynamics of the Scottish newspaper system saw the bigger cities of Edinburgh, Glasgow, Dundee and Aberdeen each with a single dominating newspaper with a wide regional sphere of influence. *The Scotsman* and *The Herald* in Glasgow (the longest-running national newspaper in the world) were considered national newspapers while other newspapers were more regional, including *The Press and Journal* in Aberdeen and *The Courier* in Dundee.

The Scotsman was the flagship publication for Scotsman Publications Ltd and it was the biggest newspaper in Scotland, owned by a Canadian company, Thompson International. *The Scotsman* was a morning paper and the *Edinburgh Evening News* was an afternoon paper, which belonged to the same media company. *The Scotsman* was founded in 1817 and its head office was a short walk from the flower-strewn gardens in the city's centre, towered over by iconic Edinburgh Castle. Daily circulation averaged 83,000 Monday to Saturday but Friday was the biggest day when it featured recruitment and sales advertising. By 2017 the audited daily print circulation had declined to 19,449 copies with a paid-for circulation of 88.3 per cent of this figure, about 17,000.

The *Edinburgh Evening News* had changed from tabloid to broadsheet the day I arrived. Its daily circulation over five editions was about 20,000, although this declined to 16,660 by February 2018.

In December 2005 Scotsman Publications was acquired in a £160 million deal by Johnston Press, a company founded in Scotland and now one of the top three largest newspaper publishers in the UK. *The Scotsman* had 119 journalists in Edinburgh and more in its Glasgow office where it competed with the *Glasgow Herald*. The paper had reporters based in London and five single-reporter offices across Scotland. *The Scotsman on Sunday* had its own separate editorial staff of about 35 journalists. In 2012, *The Scotsman* was named Newspaper of the Year at the Scottish Press Awards.

Chapter 10
Dublin, Republic of Ireland

When I arrived in Dublin, Ireland had three rival daily newspapers, the *Irish Independent*, *Irish Times* and *Irish Press*. But within a week there were only two after the *Irish Press*, a tabloid morning paper, was forced to close; this came after months of industrial upheaval had thrown hundreds out of work. The paper had been losing circulation steadily for five years. In 1995, the *Irish Independent* was Ireland's largest national newspaper with 210 journalists plus 33 freelancers. The paper had Ireland's biggest circulation of around 150,000 on weekdays and the weekend broadsheet the Sunday Independent sold 250,000 copies. However, by January 2018 weekly average 120 circulation for the *Irish Independent* had fallen to 87,673 and the *Sunday Independent* to 176,580 (News Brands Ireland).

Security Editor Tom Brady

Tom Brady was responsible for news coverage of crime, police and defence for the *Irish Independent*, Ireland's biggest newspaper Brady's news round took him to the headquarters of the Garda Siochana (Gaelic for Guardians of the Peace), the Dáil Éireann (the Irish Parliament) and out onto the streets for police and crime coverage. His relations with police were collegiate and semi-formal and police and newspapers were respectful and supportive.

But serious crime provided little by way of big news splashes or drama in Ireland. Life was not beset by armed gangs running drug operations or run-down urban enclaves of potential danger to outsiders. This helped to explain why the police-crime round could be handled as part of a bigger rounds package.

Brady was an experienced reporter and careful how he handled his police contacts. However, he relied on formal channels and this was the style used elsewhere in Europe. His associations with various police figures were built around being on good terms rather than seeking anonymous police sources.

Crime was infrequent in Ireland and serious crimes were rare events. In these circumstances there was a sense of being prepared to work as a group that was given direction by police. It was quite a positive way for police to work with the media generally and prepared to be on good terms with a senior writer like Brady. He said he was conscious there could be perceptions of being too close to the Garda, but Dublin's ease of movement and lack of serious crime opened the way to lots of informal contact.

Ireland was unique in western countries for having a single police force, the Garda Siochana. The Garda carried out all security, traffic and criminal law enforcement functions and had 8,500 uniformed police and 1,700 plain-clothes detectives. Uniformed police in Ireland did not carry firearms. The nation was divided into 23 police divisions, each commanded by a chief superintendent, with five divisions forming the Dublin metropolitan area. Altogether there were 700 police stations across the country.

There were just 23 murders across all counties of Ireland in 1993 for a population of 5.29 million, and Dublin had seven murders for a population of 1.6 million. By comparison, Chicago with 2.8 million residents had 930 homicides in 1993.

The Garda Siochana solved all but three of the 23 murders, although 12 police officers had been killed between 1970 to 1990, but for the most part these were in the context of subversive-related activities.

Cannabis was Ireland's principal illegal drug in 1993 accounting for around 3,000 of the 3,833 drug offences. The Garda had made 15 arrests for cocaine, 81 for heroin and 129 for LSD (lysergic acid diethylamide) also known as acid. Stealing was Ireland's most common crime and 60 per cent of all criminal activities took place in the Dublin metropolitan area. Nevertheless, Garda Commissioner Patrick J. Culligan (who retired in 1996) said 1993 had seen the highest rate of crime detection in a decade. The largest increases were for larcenies and property crime and car thefts had risen 39 per cent, to a total of 2,000 stolen cars for the entire country.

Ireland was unique in western countries for having a single police force, the Garda Siochana. The Garda carried out all security, traffic and criminal law enforcement functions and had 8,500 uniformed police and 1,700 plain-clothes detectives. Uniformed police in Ireland did not carry firearms. The nation was divided into 23 police divisions, each commanded by a chief superintendent, with five divisions forming the Dublin metropolitan area. Altogether there were 700 police stations across the country.

Supt. Bryan O'Higgins

Brady took me to meet the officer in charge of the Garda press and public relations office Superintendent Bryan O'Higgins, at Garda headquarters at Phoenix Park, one of the largest municipal parks in Europe. It was a picture-perfect setting reflecting the mood of largely crimeless Ireland.

There was no suggestion of pressures in the way newspapers and the Garda worked together as stories emerged. Supt. O'Higgins said the Garda press and public relations office was not beset by newspaper reporters for details of crime. But his office carried out a sophisticated program of publicising its role through media outlets and took part in police and crime campaigns on television, radio and in newspapers. One outlet was a monthly television series, *Crime-Line*, which invited the public to call in to provide tip-offs or seek assistance. He said *Crime-Line* generated around 200 phone calls for each program.

Ireland's Drug Seizures 1993

Type of drug	Quantity seized	Offenders
Cannabis resin	4,200 kilograms	2,895
Cannabis herb	975 grams	59
Cannabis plants	450	-
Cocaine	347 grams	15
Amphetamine	741 grams / 147 tablets	82
LSD	5,522	129
Morphine	4,345 tablets	53
Heroin	1,284 grams	81
Ecstasy	744 tablets	66

* Source: Garda Siochana Annual Report.

Compared with America and even with the UK Ireland was virtually crime free. Crime was unlikely to generate the deep-seated antagonism or media rivalry that surrounded crime reporting elsewhere.

Part Two
Gangs, Guns and Drugs

Most large American cities faced endemic poverty and street violence in crumbling inner-city estates in the 1990s. The same high levels of drugs and gang related killings have returned like an avenging angel, due to the widespread use of drugs like fentanyl and decades of neglect and indifference by America's political leadership and city administrations at every level. America's ability to generate massive wealth and influence has not been used to respond to this tragic collapse of civilization, within walking distance of some of the richest corporations in the world.

The rise of deadly new drugs, open borders and homelessness all combine to add an ominous chapter in this on-going collapse of inner cities into zones of chaos, danger and neglect.

Yet police were left alone to respond to this unsolvable social catastrophe, starved of funding and without adequate support and demonised – because they are the ones who must face this danger alone.

Chapter 11
Living in Fear

Fifty years ago, the United States was caught up in the Second World War. In those difficult times there was the fear of losing family and friends and even democracy itself. Today Americans are focused on different kinds of fears – crime and violence – that have become a part of everyday life. The fear of crime has settled over communities everywhere, challenging our sense of safety and law enforcement's resources. This fear alters the way we perceive ourselves, our society and law enforcement.

* United States' Department of Justice Crime Reports 1994.

The curse of illegal drugs is one of the great unspoken realities of modern societies everywhere. Very little coverage appears in the media, due largely to widespread disinterest and inertia and lack of any genuine concern by the ruling political elites, the wealthy and the heads of industry, commerce and banking. All western governments seem incapable of defending their borders from the flood of illegal migrants or the endless flow of drugs carried along the Cocaine Trail.

Most of the millions of undocumented migrants come mainly from dysfunctional societies in Latin and South America, Africa or the Middle East. They just walk across the borders or land on the beaches, claiming to be escaping persecution. Yet this exodus is a carefully orchestrated money-making industry, run by people smugglers and drug cartels and designed to provide income for criminal enterprises through drugs, illegal immigration and the movement of international criminals.

Many believe this decades-long river of people has contributed to America's cycles of violence, homicides, the drug pandemic, shooting fixation, crime, gangs, poverty and overcrowding. Millions more have poured into the overcrowded inner cities since 1995, and observed amongst them are some of the most violent criminals and hardened thugs in South America.

Cities in Latin and South America are among the most violent and lawless in the world, and they are dominated by drug cartels, who run the drugs trade and have the power to hold administrations and police at bay. Drug traffickers or gang members arrive in America hidden within the larger diaspora of genuine refugees seeking a better life. Editors and police say the flood of new arrivals places enormous stresses on schools, health services and welfare support, police, courts, and prisons. This in turn disadvantages the minority American families already struggling to survive in these large crumbling ghettos.

Homicide Rates

No democratic nation on earth has the same homicide rates as America, based on a United Nations' study of international homicides in 2018 (UN Office on Drugs and Crime). The study shows that America had 16,214 homicides, or 4.96 per 100,000 people, which is a 20.7 per cent increase since 2013. This means America's homicide rate is roughly five times worse than the next worst democratic nation in the study.

Other countries were all spectacularly lower, Canada's homicide rate was 1.76 (or 651 homicides), United Kingdom 1.2 (809 homicides), Australia 0.89 (222 homicides) and Republic of Ireland 0.87 (42 homicides).

There were 16,000 to 26,000 homicides a year in the United States from 1981 to 2009 (National Centre for Injury Prevention and Control, Morbidity and Mortality, 2013). This is more homicides on average every year than all the 19,733 US Marines who died over five years in World War II in all theatres of war.

Homicides in Major American Cities 1993 to 2017

	1993	1994	1995	2017
Seattle	67	71	48	27
San Antonio	220	94	140	151
New York City	1,946	1,571	1,182	290
San Diego	133	119	94	50
Houston	446	379	304	279
St Louis	267	248	203	203
Miami	127	129	111	93
New Orleans	395	421	364	175
Chicago	845	930	823	650
Washington	454	399	360	116
Atlanta	203	*192	145	79
Dallas	317	291	276	72
Detroit	579	525	514	267
Los Angeles	1,076	*1,119	828	282
Phoenix	158	244	244	161
Baltimore	353	321	325	343
Denver	74	85	90	28
Boston	98	85	98	42
Minneapolis	58	62	97	35

* Source: US Department of Justice / *Time Magazine*.

** Note 1: These 'real' statistics came directly from city police departments and the FBI. Atlanta and LA both issued far lower figures to the media and to *Time* Magazine.

Homicide trends and record levels of drug-related deaths confirm the extent of this national tragedy: Baltimore had 353 homicides in 2017 – this was the same as 1993 (*National Review*, December 26, 2019), Detroit had 267 homicides (not far off the record of 317 in 1993), Phoenix had 161 homicides (compared with 244 in 1994 and 244 again in 1995), and New Orleans had 175 (compared to 220 in 2022 and 424 in 1994).

Homicides ticked up again in 2021 with a 5 per cent increase from 2020 and a 44 per cent increase over 2019, according to an analysis of crime trends by the Council on Criminal Justice (CCJ). The study drew on crime data from 22 cities nationwide — including Atlanta, Detroit, Baltimore, Chicago, Denver, Memphis, San Francisco, Washington D.C. and Philadelphia. While the overall increase in homicide rates had slowed, they jumped in St. Petersburg, Florida (108 per cent) and Austin (86 per cent) while Washington D.C. also recorded a notable increase (16 per cent).

World's Ten Most Violent Cities (2017)

The sadistic violence that rages unchecked across South American cities is driven by an extensive and organised culture of drug production and trafficking by drug cartels, which control many cities. Insecurity is exacerbated by political instability, poverty, corruption and poor economic conditions. Entrenched corruption and abuses by officials also facilitate crime and violence.

Forty-two of the world's 50 most dangerous cities are in Latin America, according to a 2017 study compiled by Mexico's Citizens' Council for Public Security. Of the 42 cities in Latin America 17 are in Brazil, 12 in Mexico, five in Venezuela, three in Colombia, two in Honduras and one each in El Salvador, Guatemala, and Jamaica. These countries all have devastating levels of drugs and they also have largely corrupt governments as well.

America had only three cities on the list despite being the worst democratic nation on earth for homicides: Baltimore (listed at 21) New Orleans (41) and Detroit (42). Mexico had five cities in the top 10 including Los Cabos, judged the world's most deadly city (Business Insider Australia, March 2018).

*

1. Los Cabos (Mexico) 365 homicides, population 328,245 (a rate of 111.33 homicides per 100,000 residents).
2. Caracas (Venezuela) 3,387 homicides, population 3,046,104 (111.19 homicides per 100,000 residents).
3. Acapulco (Mexico) 910 homicides, population 853,646 (106.63 homicides per 100,000 residents).

4. Natal (Brazil) 1,378 homicides, population 1,343,573 (102.56 homicides per 100,000 residents).
5. Tijuana (Mexico) 1,897 homicides, population 1,882,492 (100.77 homicides per 100,000 residents).
6. La Paz (Mexico) 259 homicides, population 305,455 (84.79 homicides per 100,000 residents).
7. Fortaleza (Brazil) 3,270 homicides, population 3,917,279 (83.48 homicides per 100,000 residents).
8. Ciudad Victoria (Mexico) 301 homicides, population 361,078 (83.32 homicides per 100,000 residents).
9. Ciudad Guayana (Venezuela) 728 homicides, population 906,879 (80.28 homicides per 100,000 residents).
10. Belem (Brazil) 1,743 homicides, population 2,441,761 (71.38 homicides per 100,000 residents).

All cities in the study had populations greater than 300,000.

* Source: Mexico's Citizens' Council for Public Security

American Cities in the Study

21. Baltimore (USA) 341 homicides, population 614,664 (55.48 homicides per 100,000 residents).
41. New Orleans (USA) 157 homicides, population 391,495 (40.10 homicides per 100,000 residents).
42. Detroit (USA) 267 homicides, population 672,795 (39.69 homicides per 100,000 residents).

Turning Point in History

Cocaine first arrived in America in large volumes in 1986, derived from the coca plant in Colombia, Peru and Bolivia. Like all illicit drugs, the bulk of it crosses the border with Mexico and is then distributed via gang networks to every street corner on the North American continent. This is the world's most lucrative black market for illicit drugs, including the entire family of opioids. In recent years cocaine has been overtaken by the far more deadly and addictive fentanyl, with the precursors manufactured in Chinese laboratories.

Cocaine is a powerfully addictive stimulant drug made from the leaves of the coca plant that is native to South America. It resembles a fine white crystal powder and is often mixed with corn starch, talcum powder or flour to increase profits. It can also be mixed with stimulant amphetamine or synthetic opioids, including fentanyl. Adding synthetic opioids to cocaine is especially dangerous because users have no way of knowing about these additives. Rapidly rising overdose deaths are related to this tampered cocaine.

Drug users snort cocaine powder through the nose or rub it into their gums. Others dissolve it to inject it into the bloodstream. Some inject a combination of cocaine and heroin – a Speedball. But the most popular method is to smoke cocaine that has been processed to make a rock crystal (also called freebase cocaine). The crystal is heated to produce vapours, then inhaled into the lungs. This is crack cocaine, which refers to the crackling sound of the rock as it's heated. Some smoke crack by sprinkling it on marijuana or tobacco and smoke it like a cigarette.

People who use cocaine often have binges – taking the drug repeatedly within a short time at increasingly higher doses to maintain their high. Cocaine increases levels of the natural chemical messenger dopamine in brain circuits, impairing moods, movement, and reward. Many users will never feel happiness again. For users everywhere, cocaine is the Angel of Death.

Fentanyl

The vast illegal drugs industry once based on heroin and cocaine has morphed into the even more evil family of synthetic opioids, predominantly fentanyl. This deadly drug is made from base chemicals manufactured in Chinese laboratories, often with government subsidies (How Chemists, Chinese Factories, and "Dark Web" Dealers Spread Fentanyl Across the US, *The Nation*, December 2019).

However, by 2021 drug overdose deaths had spiked to 107,735, primarily from fentanyl, and a 50 per cent jump in only five years (Fox News January 20, 2022). Of these, 71,238 were from fentanyl. It is also an increase of 15 per cent from 93,655 deaths in 2020 or roughly five times the national homicide rate, which stood at 19,600 in 2021.

Drug Type	Deaths 2021	Deaths 2020
Synthetic Opioids (fentanyl)	71,238	57,834
Psychostimulants (meth)	32,856	24,576
Cocaine	24,856	19,927
Natural/semi-synthetic (pres)	13,503	13,722

* Source: CDC, National Center for Health Statistics

An even more appalling scenario lies ahead, with more than 1.2 million additional opioid overdose deaths now expected in North America by 2029 (Medical Press).

Drug-Induced Homelessness

The spread of drugs across American society has spawned a culture of drug-related homelessness, with discarded humans subsisting in flimsy street encampments across inner-city business districts with nowhere else to go. Millions of Americans have been dislocated from mainstream life because of drug-induced mental illness, joblessness, pointlessness, and hopelessness.

On a given night in 2018 there was an estimated 553,000 homeless people in America, or 0.17 per cent of the population (US Department of Housing and Urban Development's Annual Homeless Assessment Report).

High-crime cities like Los Angeles, Baltimore and San Francisco now face this worsening phenomenon. Many commercial zones once immune to the social decay of the inner-cities are now plagued by trash, drugs, violent and drug-affected people and untreated sewage on the streets. Many desperate business owners face the prospect of these people living in front of their high-profile offices, showrooms and reception areas, killing business and driving away customers. It doesn't help that nearby inner-city ghettos are home to armed gangs where drugs are plentiful.

Chapter 12
Street Gangs

FBI studies show the extent to which gangs continue to dominate all crime in America today, masterminding most of the drug trafficking and prostitution, car theft networks, armed robberies, and assassinations and counter assassinations. They are behind the national rise in homicides as well, according to police in numerous cities. They flourish in run-down and disorganised inner-city estates where fresh recruits are widely available. Almost all of them are products of dysfunctional single-parent families, a feature of life in these forgotten estates. Some newspaper gang specialists described young new recruits as 'loveless children' who are seeking a sense of belonging and hope in their downtrodden worlds.

Yet few media outlets give any national emphasis to this urban disaster staring them in the face.

Gangs are becoming more violent while engaging in less typical and lower-risk crime such as prostitution and white-collar crime. Gangs are more adaptable, organised, sophisticated, and opportunistic, exploiting new and advanced technology as a means to recruit, communicate discreetly, target their rivals, and perpetuate their criminal activity.

* Source: the FBI

The arrival of crack cocaine after 1986 spurred the expansion of gang networks in all major cities in the United States. Children are recruited from impoverished public housing estates, and they soon learn to use sophisticated weapons in the endless wars over drug turf. Street gangs are the youthful foot soldiers for national criminal networks run by gang chieftains from inside prisons. They terrorise public housing estates across the nation and almost all of them are enlisted from struggling minority families and immigrants, who live on the outer edges of civilization in crumbling slum housing. Combined, these factors have pushed much of America into an age of fear.

There were more than 400,000 street gang members in America in 1995, according to my newspaper research, studies by the FBI and police in Los Angeles and Chicago. These were America's worst cities for gang violence – although Florida and New York come close. National gang membership surged to an estimated 1.4 million by 2011 comprising more than 33,000 street gangs, motorcycle gangs and prison gangs nationwide (National Gang Threat Assessment, Emerging Trends, National Gang Intelligence Centre 2011; and What We Investigate, Gangs, FBI).

The gangs continue to be a force in all criminal activities in 2023, recruiting new members from urban, suburban and rural regions across America. They are tangible criminal associations and their chief aim is to expand their influence over street-level drug sales. The most notable trend in 2011 was the overall increase in gang membership, greater control of street-level drug sales and collaboration with rival gangs and other criminal organisations.

They have continued expanding and evolving and pose an existential threat to American communities nationwide. Many are sophisticated criminal networks with members who are violent who distribute wholesale quantities of drugs and who develop and maintain close working relationships with transnational criminal / drug trafficking organisations.

Gangs in Chicago

Ernest Di Benedetto, the supervisor of the Gang Prosecutions Unit of Chicago's Cook County state attorney's office, said:

It's no longer like *West Side Story* where six kids from one area get together and slug it out with six kids from another. Gangs today routinely use guns and knives. They have many young members who lack maturity and who would think nothing of taking a pistol and going out and shooting somebody over a sweater.

Chicago had an estimated 58,000 to 100,000 gang members in 1995 and more and younger recruits were signing on every day. *Chicago Tribune* bureau chief Bill Recktenwald told me most of these kids were on a one-way conveyor belt to crime, prison or death.

Many were drawn to gangs in the first place through loneliness and were really seeking affection and closeness. He said the gangs with their high idealism and hard rules filled an emotional void for boys from poor homes who accepted the danger, yet the truth is they craved love and belonging. It was difficult for outsiders to comprehend a gang culture that spawned in inner-city slums like Chicago's West Side or the wastelands of Los Angeles.

Gang-Related Crime 1993

Homicides	129
Drive-by shootings	177
Armed robberies	533
Aggravated sexual assaults	9
Serious assaults	3,221
Drug offences	8,842

* Source: Chicago Police Department

The *Chicago Tribune* produced a book to define and explain the gang phenomenon. It uncovered a startling subculture that dominates minority neighbourhoods and lower-class white neighbourhoods in what may truly be called the most American of all cities. In these run-down parts of Chicago, it was the street gang not the alderman or the policeman that had the clout. And their scope of control was mindboggling stretching from gun-toting teenagers who charged for protection to middle-aged gang leaders who have become slum landlords and drug-ring kings.

Street gangs are a major cultural and economic force in the community in Chicago. Their background, power and emerging political influence are the reasons for efforts to define the changing face of organised crime.

Commander Donald Hilbring of the Gang Investigation Unit (passed in 2009) told me there were between 30,000 to 50,000 hard-core gang members in Chicago. But 'wannabes' and marginal members boosted membership to more than 100,000. The wider area known as Chicagoland had around 125 gangs in large areas of Cook, Kane, DuPage, Will and Lake counties. The Cook County Sheriff's Gangs' Unit tracked 58 satellite gangs operating in their suburbs.

*

This is the downtrodden and violent world of street gangs with their iconic labels as Crips and Bloods or Folks and the People. Their lives are dominated by crime since childhood and the rule of gang law is always about violence. These wayward children grow up in a ferocious pattern of savagery where guns do all the talking and no-one is safe. They are a product of downtrodden, squalid estates, hidden from view and abandoned in the decaying inner cities.

The most frequent witnesses to these dangerous places are the police, who face this dark side of human nature largely on their own. Their one-time allies in this perilous environment were the police reporters, dedicated loners from traditional printed newspapers searching for the best and worst of life and death. For decades the ghettos in America were the new frontier but the dust has settled on their long-term relationship, eroded by time, societal change and distrust. Police increasingly are targeted as brutal, racist or corrupt. However, these often-over-hyped slogans are part of a wider resentment against authority, an undeclared social war to dismantle long-held assumptions about racism or about who has the right to wealth, privilege or control.

Folks and the People

Over the years Latino, African American, Asian and white gangs merged into two major gang groupings in Chicago known as the Folks and the People. This deal was hammered out inside the jails and the alliances were respectfully maintained on the streets where bitter and murderous rivalries exist. The People wear distinctive clothing, hats with visors to the left side, earrings in the left ear, left shoe tied a certain way and the pant leg cuffed on the left side. The Folks wear their identifiers in the reverse fashion and are instantly recognizable to their own and other gangs. Hand signs are widely used and always given in the 'up' position and a hand signal in a 'down' position is a gesture of disrespect that will lead to retaliation or shootings.

The Black Gangster Disciples (also called the BGDs) was Chicago's largest and most lethal street gang with mainly African American membership. In 1995 the BGDs had between 18,000 and 25,000 members and ran satellite operations in other mid-western communities. In Chicago the gang operated mainly on the South Side and controlled two-thirds of the city's low-income housing developments. The BGDs familiar crossed pitchfork emblem and six-pointed star (the Star of David) were spray-painted on public buildings, rail platforms and residences. Approximately 8,000 BGD gang members were arrested between 1989 and 1990 but the gang's criminal activities were not reduced or curtailed.

The Gang Book

The Chicago Crime Commission said in the 'Gang Book' that gang leaders attracted and recruited disenfranchised youths at various ages offering them important sources of identity and alternatives. Gangs become their extended families providing them with companionship, money and clothing, powerful lures for the products of broken homes and single-parent households (see Gangs, Wikipedia).

The initiation process takes the form of a violent act against a rival faction and the new member's reputation is quickly assessed. It is weighed against the amount of money he can bring into the gang or how successfully he carries out the kill when ordered to do so by the leader. Membership status is earned over time unless the member dies in the process. Fallen members are accorded a gang holiday in which the gang sweater and colours are displayed on the casket and in the gang clubhouse. Gangs are hierarchical and new members' first duties are acting as lookouts for police squad cars during narcotics transactions, burglaries or guarding entrances to buildings, as I saw at the Robert Taylor Homes. Leadership usually depends on mental toughness, a logical train of thought and propensity for instant violence. Gang leaders are extremely violent and members who break gang rules receive swift retaliation with beatings or execution. A leader or 'King of the Nation' expects results.

A commission report on the city's gang infrastructure found that in 1973 only 3 per cent of all homicides were related to street gangs. But by 1993 that ratio had grown to 15 per cent and then to 34 per cent by 1994. In 1990 12,153 gang members were in prison but by 1993 17,489 were behind bars. Chicago Police recorded 129 gang-on-gang killings in 1993, the second-highest number since police began recording gang assassinations 26 years before. Of the 129 homicides 125 involved guns.

The death toll in 1991 set a record where 133 killings were attributed to gangs mostly over territorial disputes. The gun was the weapon of choice in almost all gang-related homicides using high-calibre armament or automatic or semi-automatic weapons.

Robert J. Simandl, a gang crime specialist with the Chicago Police Department, said quiet communities were good covers for gangs wanting to branch out to new locations where they rented apartments to store drugs and weapons. "No matter where you live, gangs are apt to come through your area," he said.

Gangs were not confined to African American or Latino areas either but they were in every area of the city and suburbs, according to Catherine Ryan, the chief prosecutor for Cook County Juvenile Court. She said the growth of gangs was "the worst thing in this city and people don't realise how bad it is and how bad it is getting."

Newspaper Gang Specialist

Gangs have a growing presence and reputation in Chicago with a recognisable character and a defined place in society, albeit a run-down and poorer corner of it. George Papajohn, a street gang specialist for the *Chicago Tribune,* said it was the job of newspapers to identify and expose the gangs and gang leaders for what they were and not to shirk from this for fear of radiating publicity about crime and criminals. Not knowing who they were left the public more vulnerable and unsuspecting. "People should know who the urban terrorists are, who the leaders are and how they operate, and who it is destroying their communities."

Newspapers should not ignore the problems in the society they reported on and news coverage did not seek to turn murderers into heroes. They were heroes already in their own communities and had the trappings of wealth, with cars, money and girls yet they had little impact on the wider society. Papajohn said he strived to enlighten the community but he did not rely on police department sources. He avoided putting forward only a police viewpoint and would meet with local and federal law agents and people from the community and community agencies, who generally knew more about gangs than police anyway.

From time-to-time Papajohn would meet up with gang members being careful to have a trustworthy intermediary who asked the gang member to speak openly without fear of having his identity revealed. He often asked social workers to persuade recycled gang members to speak to him about gang life, symbols, territories, codes and dress.

Many homicides still came from a spousal or lovers spat and there were still random acts of violence. However, children became victims wherever guns were available, particularly handguns. There was a reasonable fear that anything could happen, and gangs of Crips or Bloods would end up in your town, turning it into a bloody battleground over drug territory. Most Americans did not fit the profiles for danger and they could expect to be reasonably safe from violent crime and homicide. "It still depends on where you live, what you do and how you run your life," Papajohn said.

The *Chicago Tribune's* massive effort to expose child homicides would not have a speedy impact but it would contribute and perhaps lead to a better understanding of the problem. "You can't measure what we've done [just] by numbers."

Chapter 13
Firearms

New Gun Every 20 Seconds

America was going through the most violent period in its history with growing sophistication of weaponry and increasingly younger offenders and victims. Young people had access to hi-tech automatic weapons but this was not what the Second Amendment was designed for. It was meant to provide a home militia against an overseas oppressor.

Firearm ownership is one of the most emotional issues in America, according to Jerry Singer, a special agent for the Bureau of Tobacco, Alcohol and Firearms, a branch of the US Treasury Department. He said gun ownership in America had increased almost five times since 1950 when there were 50 million guns. This doubled to 100 million in 1970 and by 1990 there was an estimated 200 million guns in America. By 1995 there were 220 to 230 million guns including 67 million handguns, and they were the most negotiable item of trade on the streets after narcotics. Agent Singer said manufacturers made a further 1.5 million handguns in 1994 alone – one every 20 seconds.

The Chicago Police Department's annual homicide analysis in 1993 showed that handguns were increasingly the primary weapon used in homicides. Handguns were used in 158 homicides in 1965 but by 1993 handgun killings in Chicago had risen to 551. The percentage of gun-related homicides went from 49 per cent in 1965 to 74 per cent in 1993. Of 845 homicides in 1993, 629 involved guns (328 were semi-automatics), 152 were large-calibre 9-millimeter guns, rifles were used in nine, shotguns in 13, and unknown gun types in 64. Knives were used in 45 homicides and feet, hands and fists in 47 others.

Police once used six-shot revolvers but by the 1990s they were no longer a match for the firepower on the streets and 90 per cent of agencies began moving to semi-automatic guns with larger clips and quicker reloading times. "More and more criminals want to hold court out on the streets," Agent Singer said. "They want to take action and do business out on the streets. It's out there. Talk is cheap on the streets but with a gun you get respect."

Chicago Police Chief

Chicago police chief, Superintendent Matt Rodriguez was chairman of the Major Cities Chiefs Forum, which comprised 45 American police districts plus four from Canada. He was the most senior police chief in North America and resolutely opposed to guns in the wrong hands and access to firearms was the biggest threat to law and order in America.

"It is firearms," Supt. Rodriguez said. They were conveniently at hand when people got into heated situations and they led to a greater number of suicides.

The availability of guns put police officers in direct conflict with large well-armed private armies who resorted to guns at every opportunity. "We must do whatever we can to stop youth from being delinquent but keeping guns out of society is essential."

Police in cities across America now accepted that gun violence had become 'normalised' and a part of life. The aftershocks of multiple shooting deaths out on the projects almost every night were no longer as great as they had been 20 years or even 40 years before. This was blamed on a combination of routine and indifference but it was really normalisation. It was generally accepted that 18- to 19-year-olds could obtain guns although the law says they should be 21. Offenders and their victims were getting younger too and it took a shooting by an 8- or 9-year-old to raise public concern.

Supt. Rodriguez said the shooting of a 14-year-old the day before in Chicago's poor West Side was a perfect example of how the justice system failed to work. The youth would be paralysed for life and he would need enormously expensive medical care and welfare support. Yet the manufacturer of the gun would have to pay nothing. Nor would the National Rifle Association, which lobbied constantly to free up gun laws. Nothing would be asked of the person who legally bought the gun used to shoot the youth. "But the rest of society will pay. The cost of emergency hospital care and welfare for the rest of the teenager's life would be incalculable. As for our future unless we curtail access to weapons or change the mindset of young people it could get worse."

He said the National Rifle Association was comprised of 'men in striped suits and ties' who represented manufacturers and whose only interest was in selling weapons. Socioeconomic factors had contributed but "what does that mean, and what can we do about it?"

Supt. Rodriguez said the situation facing police was frightening. "You think you've reached the apex then you find another pinnacle the pro-weapons [lobby] wants to achieve." Congress seemed to be concentrating its efforts on getting more prison space. While police supported the moves, they believed something had to be done for the 40 million American children under the age of 10 to keep them off the criminal path. "I have not seen as much concern [as now] for preventive programs for children by chiefs of police."

Chicago police and city officials said illegal guns were flowing into the city unchecked and the crime statistics appeared to support their fears. A vast reservoir of illegally and legally obtained handguns existed on the streets and in 1994 police seized 23,000 to 25,000 guns. This was more than any other police jurisdiction in the country, higher even than New York or a seizure of 12,000 guns by the Los Angeles Police Department. Police had recovered only 8,300 illegal guns in 2016 and this was a 20 per cent increase on the previous year.

He blamed the information explosion, which had contributed to droves of people leaving high school for dead-end jobs or not to work at all. They faced a future without hope and were surely bound to become problems for police to have to deal with. Getting them back to school would help the police task in years to come. It was more important now for both parents to be working for a better way of life. This in turn led to a generation of 'latch-key children' who went home from schools and had to entertain themselves. Values had fallen over the last 30 years:

It took 35 years for us to get where we are at and for narcotics to be important and weapons a debilitating scourge on society. It's going to take time to turn it around. Do we press a button? It's not going to happen this way.

There was a great movement by individuals who felt afraid for their safety and they would rather be armed. "Do you know what it would be like if everyone was armed?" To emphasize this point he said a recent shooting on a railway car where six people were killed and 19 injured could have been far worse if passengers shot back in a crowded railway carriage. Police already faced charges of not closely following laws on the use of deadly force and killing bystanders in stressful situations. They were trained and tested twice a year to be proficient in using firearms, but the public would not be even remotely as trained or efficient.

Historically, the problem had its beginnings in the 1960s, an era that was the genesis of the drug problem. Previously held American values were put to one side, such as the family and education, and they were relegated to the back burner. A crime study ordered by President Lyndon B. Johnson in the mid-1960s which was carried out by a commission delivered a report called *Crime and Violence in a Free Society*. "The major concern then was the availability of firearms. We are still trying to stop making them available to the general populace."

It was ironic that the *Time-Newsweek* coverage of the Colombian Medellin drug cartels in the 1960s portrayed that country as very violent with well-armed thugs and lots of cocaine for sale. They were all young and had little regard for human life. "Today somebody could read that in Australia about the USA. That was exactly how things were in the 11th police district on the West Side of Chicago. I hope you in Australia do not have to say that about Australia ten years down the line. I hope you are still shocked by homicides."

Supt. Rodriguez said the Cold War had been a major concern in America at the time but its place had been taken by fear of crime. This focus on crime might lead to solutions but he said America sometimes needed a Pearl Harbour. Crime problems in cities like Chicago or New Orleans were older than just a couple of years. Their large project areas and satellite townships where mostly poor black people lived were badly designed and invited trouble. Anyone placing thousands of poor families into 24-storey buildings could expect things to get worse. Many children were in single-parent families without fathers and they were vulnerable to the influences around them.

The situation in Chicago was worse even than New York where at least poorer people lived with others from different backgrounds than their own. "Here we have nothing but those who are absolutely poor and unable to hold a job. If they get a job they disqualify themselves from being there, it is exacerbated." Other cities like New Orleans faced police corruption problems as well as high crime rates. This was made worse by the poor pay for police, forcing them to act as bouncers and guards for local clubs or casinos. Many of these employers were more powerful and offered better pay than the city and gave incentives for police to seek better income.

He said police chiefs in America supported President Clinton's Crime Bill, *Violent Crime Control and Law Enforcement Act,* which became law in 1994 and was the largest crime bill in American history. But many Congressmen were surprised at police interest in getting preventive programs in place for youth and to get school dropouts back to school.

Supt. Rodriguez said he had an open-door policy to the press and he tried to be as cooperative as he could, but he was concerned about the media's concentration on violence and sensationalism, which he put down to heavy competition in Chicago by competing newspapers. Many saw Chicago as having the most aggressive press in the country and the press saw policing as a good area to cover but it tended to sensationalise. Police coverage made a big deal of some issues but did not report fewer volatile issues on the same scale. He said modern-day police chiefs were a product of the sixties, seventies and eighties:

We are the ones who filled all the jails and we can do it again so fast your head would spin but we need to do something more. Maybe we should have done it differently. I don't purport to have the answers.

Part Three
Crime Reporters

American police and crime reporters are probably the best investigative journalists in the world. Their crime and police coverage gave papers great drama, immediacy, accuracy, action, colour and explanations. They were the gift that kept on giving. But once they began to paint a disconcerting portrait of life in America, crime lost its news interest, with a focus on degraded inner cities where gangs, drugs and homicides were out of control. Newspapers began to set their sights on more varied and entertaining content for a middle-class readership. The drugs and guns carnage didn't let up, but crime desks around the world were cutting back on crime coverage and crime depth soon began to die. These were the worst years for homicides ever experienced, yet one by one newspapers simply stopped reporting them.

The routine homicides around inner-city housing estates began to lose their appeal and only a few of the worst or more awe-inspiring were getting to page 1 or even reported at all. Old-style police reporters who once dedicated their lives to this cause were not essential anymore. At first, reporters relied on a web of police informants, who collaborated with them in putting together crime stories on the basis of anonymity. But by the early 1990s their stories had fallen out of step with new corporate guidelines. Newspapers broadened the crime desks to include non-specialist reporters who had no allegiance to the police cause, and who were being assigned stories by editorial staff. They were unable to reproduce the rich insights into crime coverage that was only possible when it came from a police perspective. Their stories also began to probe behind the blue code, into police corruption, racism, bullying and poor performance, which led to a new fracture line between the institutions of police and newspapers.

At this point, far fewer newspapers in America and across the English-speaking world had any serious interest in covering crime and were aiming for lighter news content. In short, it was the start of the end of the road for crime reporting.

This has led to a decline in the breadth and depth of crime coverage, now marked by indifference and disinterest. As newspapers went into retreat once the internet came to dominate world information systems, they found themselves in a new battle for survival. Crime coverage now comes from hand-outs from police media units, social media, Facebook or Twitter or random calls from bystanders. Journalism has vanished into a black hole of bloggers and scammers and on-line pirate news outlets on YouTube. Relations with police are even more impersonal, distant and unproductive.

Chapter 14
Police Reporters

Traditional police reporting is a unique stream of investigative journalism that arose in America to deliver the most graphic crime coverage in the world. A national obsession with crime splashes was enhanced by a revolution in page layout in 1887 with the introduction of half-tone pictures, plus eye-catching typography and bold multi-stack headlines.

Next came Yellow Journalism – a bitterly contested newspaper rivalry from 1895 to 1898 between Joseph Pulitzer's bitterly contested newspaper rivalry from 1895 to 1898 – between Joseph Pulitzer's *New York World* and William Randolph Hearst's *New York Journal*. The idea was to sensationalise news to drive up circulation by any means possible, and the media industry was highly competitive with most cities having two or three major newspapers battling each other for ratings.

Yellow Journalism sacrificed many essential standards of journalism, such as accuracy, truthfulness, impartiality and fairness solely to drive up sales. Yellow Journalism is widely blamed for influencing the 1898 Spanish-American War over Cuba as part of this same hubris. Hearst was also accused of calling for the assassination of President William McKinley in an editorial (the President was assassinated soon afterwards on September 14, 1901). Yellow Journalism galvanised newspapers across America, seeking to compete with their city rivals for coverage of big breaking stories.

Media Offices in Police Stations

For many of the early to mid-decades of the twentieth century, metropolitan newspapers and national media networks enjoyed a unique and long-standing collaboration with operational police and detectives.

Until the 1980s most big city news outlets and media networks in America worked out of offices inside police stations. They would be able to accompany the police response out to crime scenes where they could get graphic details, interview witnesses and get pictures from the scene. Crime stories soon began to dominate front page headlines, especially during the brutal era of the Mafia, the archetypes of murder, assassination and crime. Access to breaking crime scenes was automatic and operational police were willing to share details of their investigations with the press. It was the start of dedicated police roundsmen on news desks. Crime scenes were always presented in great detail and police shown in a positive light. This drama spilled over into television series and movies with the crooks pursued by intrepid police. Police like Eliot Ness became household names during the prohibition era and newspapers and the readers lapped it up. Circulation soared.

This proximity to newspaper reporters gave police great influence in shaping crime stories and using the media to dig out evidence for their investigations. News outlets happily cooperated. It was a quid pro quo and no-one in the media was asking whether it affected impartiality or held police to account. Nor did they explain to readers the exact nature of this cloying proximity to police.

Crime Round Evolves

America had been experiencing nationwide civil rights riots since the 1960s, culminating in the assassination of Martin Luther King in 1968. The country's social structure was in a state of dramatic change and the once widespread arrangement of working from inside police stations was starting to break down through mutual suspicion and distrust. Old-style police reporting and in-bed relations with the cops were disappearing from the scene in a dynamic America.

Eventually, newspapers began calling their police reporters 'crime reporters' and this was to become one of the most important rounds on any newspaper. It was more sensitive to wide-ranging scandals involving police, yet it retained close ties with police investigations. A lot of papers retained the police round however, but newspapers had begun putting a bit more distance between themselves and police departments.

Reporters retained their effectiveness by building ties of loyalty and trust with operational police and detectives. They were getting early tipoffs and factual details and colour from crime scenes. It was all based on newspapers protecting police anonymity so individual officers can provide plenty of detail to newspapers and avoid any retribution. This instantly propelled newspapers into the front line of crime coverage. No television or radio station had such extensive news desks as newspapers and only the very largest could afford a dedicated crime reporter. This handed newspapers leadership of crime coverage everywhere, and that was still unchallenged by the mid-1990s.

However, the gloss came off this arrangement once ambitious crime reporters began to dig behind the blue code for the biting stories departments usually wanted to avoid. Crime reporters needed to develop a keen sense of what they should avoid in order to keep their jobs and this was done by avoiding stories that were critical to police. Crime reporters dominated newspaper crime coverage in the mid-1990s and they were producing graphic stories from breaking crime scenes. But newspaper interest in covering violence and crime began to fade once homicides reached record levels and became associated with armed gangs fighting over the drugs trade. Editors knew that most of the violence was from the downtrodden world of poor minority families living in overcrowded and crime infested inner city neighbourhoods.

Not surprisingly, interest in covering serious crime began to erode away as newspapers concentrated on the interests of their middle-class readership and their dependence on advertising revenue. America had already sunk into decades of nationwide civil unrest and major newspapers found it difficult to be seen to be defending the police cause over claims of brutality and racism.

When Homicide no Longer Qualified as News

By the time I began my travels across America, newspaper editors were already seriously distracted by the worsening scale of the killings and shootings in their cities, for which they were unable to give context or explanation. They did not want to keep reporting the same things repeatedly and the many newspaper crime campaigns had achieved nothing.

Newspaper editors began to recognise that shootings and gang killings were not 'unusual' anymore. Instead, they were the new normal. On-going street feuds between junkies, drug pushers or gangs were just 'background noise' and incidents like drive-by shootings where no-one died did not capture news interest. They were no longer automatic page 1 news.

The once mutually beneficial arrangement between newspapers and police was beginning to fade – and the newspaper industry found itself at a crossroad. Homicides had been breaking records in major cities since 1989 and they were witnessing the highest homicide rates in America's history. It was an undeclared national crisis tearing cities apart, overwhelming police and turning inner city ghettos into war zones. But newspaper efforts to expose this growing phenomenon had failed to interest the political elites or lead to any reforms. And the majority middle-class readership was tiring of endlessly being reminded of the dangerous inner cities.

America's influential metropolitan newspapers turned their backs on their traditional closeness with police, and they have joined their colleagues in other countries by shrinking the extent of crime coverage as well. This in turn contributes to a widespread lack of public awareness of the extent and depth of crime, drugs and poverty, hidden in plain sight in all cities.

Who can blame newspapers for an unwillingness to keep on covering the violent breakdown of society when there is no political response? The worsening extent of violence, poverty, the drugs culture and gangs is an undeclared national disaster. Yet it has continued to this day.

The worst crimes are discarded as not really interesting enough to merit news coverage. Offenders are sometimes portrayed as occasional renegades going off the rails and straying into crime, yet criminal violence and theft have become a way of life for millions. Many have no other choices when entire estates are controlled by armed gangs, who offer the only law and justice and are the only access to income for poor kids. Violence is endemic across squalid, ethnically diverse neighbourhoods in most, if not all, American cities.

There is a global indifference to crime. All western countries now coexist with worsening, spreading cloud of property crime that supports a vast black market in drugs. This apotheosis is driven by a global surge in drug trafficking, overdose deaths and homelessness. Yet for the most part, crime has become invisible and is being whitewashed from history.

Beginning of the End

The chaos of gangs, guns and drugs began to seriously transform America in the early 1990s. The ghettos became dangerous hunting grounds for crime reporters, with endless killings and shootings across inner-city housing estates. News budget conferences had a rich source of breaking crime stories at hand for every edition. Yet solitary crime reporters were often the single point of contact with operational police. Not surprisingly, they developed great skills in managing how to provide 24-hour coverage. But this did give them an aura of being valued oddballs who could always find ways to get police to talk about anything. This was also a time for media exposés about police racism, brutality and corruption. Yet newspapers everywhere were already abandoning serious crime and most homicides never saw the light of day. This was happening in cities where homicide rates were highest, creating a false dawn that violence was declining when it was the worst police had ever experienced.

Newspapers routinely avoided telling their readers the truth about where the stories were coming from as well, and this was another breakdown of faith and one more fracture line with police. They would set up generalist news desks but call them crime desks, using writers who had no allegiance to police and had not worked with them before. The best example of this was *The Atlanta Journal-Constitution*, where reporters sidestepped police to seek out other sources from elsewhere across the criminal justice spectrum. The *Los Angeles Times* changed crime coverage into an on-going examination of the performance of the L.A.P.D. In many ways this was the beginning of the end of old-style crime reporting.

'Street-Savvy Wise-Ass'

American writer John Katz captured the transformation from traditional police reporting to solo crime reporters, to setting up crime desks with several generalist writers. He said traditional old-style police reporters had been dying out for years. The urban police reporter was perhaps the most mythologised figure of modern journalism, 'that tough-talking street-savvy wise-ass who matched cops drink for drink and wisecrack for wisecrack and who got a rewrite from *Sweetheart*'. He sets the scene for understanding what makes them tick in 'Covering the Cops' (*Criminal Justice Review,* February 1993, see John Katz, Wikipedia).

Katz pointed to the ways old-style police reporters and police usually found common ground. Coming most likely from a working-class background, he identified with and protected the men he covered, becoming their ideological comrade-in-arms rather than watchdog or chronicler. Rarely did he report on police racism, brutality and corruption, and therefore for middle-class America such evils hardly existed.

The stereotypical police reporter has virtually vanished from the country's newsrooms while the police are often shown to be corrupt, brutal and bigoted. Katz said today's upper middle-class college-educated journalists had little in common with the police and were frequently to the left of them politically.

Increasingly though, police are isolated, abandoned by journalists and everyone else as they try to deal with horrifying levels of social decay, hatred and bloodshed.

"They seem to have turned inward, talking to and trusting no-one but their lawyers and each other." Katz highlighted the television series *Cops,* and how this live time portrayal of police was a barely disguised attempt to win back public confidence. Police had never been able to plug the gap successfully once their trusted police reporter was gone, when they were faced with a sharp-eyed young reporter with no interest in being recruited to the police cause.

Special personal attributes were needed to become an effective force with networks of veteran police – a reputation for honesty and fairness and the respect of their own newspaper. This took years and it needed a whole range of rare capabilities to create a police reporter. But Katz said newspapers no longer had the patience or inclination to break in a new police reporter from the old school. Editors were not looking for that anymore, preferring slickness and impartiality.

Mitch Gelman, Crime Scene

There's a price to be paid for the relentless exposure to tragedy, especially during the worst years of America's homicide crisis after 1989. *New York Newsday* crime reporter, Mitch Gelman, revealed the impact the cycle of homicide call-outs was having on him day-after-day in his 1994 book, *Crime Scene.* Gelman was a rookie reporter trying to establish himself with veteran police inside the New York Police Department. It was the height of New York's worst years for street crime with up to 2,000 homicides recorded in a single year.

But the rules of the crime game were always changing and just out of reach for Gelman. Police told him he should follow 'Italian Rules' but then he realised this meant there were no rules. He had to coax or persuade police to give him a few lines of copy instead of rival reporters as he tried to break stories and find the best yarns for a highly demanding *Newsday* crime desk. A homicide on its own was not enough to get his news copy into the paper. He always had to find something extra, some fresh angle to give his story the edge. Mostly his reports ended up as briefs when he was cut down to size by sub-editors.

Gelman was always on the move. He hardly ever rested on his dashes from crime scene to crime scene in a quest to find something extra. But no matter how he tried he was gradually worn down by the pressure and exposure to so much death.

Covering death was debilitating as well as intoxicating and caused my mood to change as frequently as the weather. On sunny days I'd take walks in the park to escape the killing or throw a softball around with one of the other reporters or photographers at the paper. On grey days, there was no way out. The East River reminded me of industrial strips along the Rhine and the glittering and glamorous city looked like someone had painted it with a damp cloth dipped in sludge.

Crime reporting was based on unspoken lore, unbreakable contracts that were never put down on paper or signed for. The rules came down to such things as a shared vision, friendships, fundamental beliefs in what was right and wrong or what was in the public interest. It was built upon the manipulation of all available police sources in the interests of getting access to the best stories and information by any means possible.

Gelman had to find ways to operate behind police smokescreens, a blue code which demanded that cops close ranks to outsiders. The skill was to win them over with personal mannerisms, persuasive writing techniques and by projecting inside stories on police life, that otherwise would not be told. A veil of unwritten codes was widely used to break through the arctic police ice. But no prisoners were taken when the feud erupted onto the news pages.

Gelman puts into words the pulsating rhythm that faces all crime and police reporters in America. He faced unrelenting pressure to be in touch and find ways to prise the facts from police and the deals he must fashion to cultivate informants. As a rookie reporter on *Newsday*, a newspaper with a daily circulation of more than 700,000 Gelman had to find ways to survive for as long as he could before he was burnt out, blacklisted by the cops or before he too became another forgotten victim down on the East Side.

Chapter 15
Crime Bloodhounds

Crime reporting evolved to become slicker, more subtle and secretive than traditional police reporting. Newspapers were taking a step back from the appearance of being too close to police, but still no-one told readers how crime stories were really being obtained. This latest style of crime reporting involved a single switched-on reporter with a hard-fought retinue of police informants, which took years and great efforts to set up. The right personal attributes were needed to be accepted into the police inner circle. Not surprisingly they tended to be very like the police themselves. Uppermost was a shared sense of trust and similar views about crime and justice and the world in general. Police would hand out tip-offs, details and colour from crime scenes but only to those they trusted.

It was all entirely informal and though it breached regulations for some police departments, most were turning a blind eye unless stories strayed into their darker secrets. But effective crime reporters soon began to unmask other police misdeeds as well, in a rush to deliver impartial coverage of police and crime.

Crime reporting became a highly effective way of getting close to breaking crime stories giving colour and detail. As Katz said, this called for a sophisticated set of personal skills to penetrate police ranks and win the trust and respect of veteran serving officers. They also needed to satisfy a sceptical newspaper editor's desire for a public perception of impartiality. This can be a very lonely journey with many pitfalls for the unwary if confidences are broken or ignored.

Yet crime reporting had become a highly effective method for all major newspapers by the 1990s and it gave advantages over rival papers and television in the extent of factual detail, colour and impact. There was nothing even remotely similar in other western democracies, where I found relations with police to be formal, unfriendly, and colourless.

Walt Philbin, New Orleans

Walt Philbin was the right person in the right place at the right time in the violent birthplace of jazz, and he relied on a web of trusted, anonymous police contacts. This made it possible for him to follow issues behind the police blue code and dig out crookedness. Over the years, Philbin had developed sophisticated tactics to avoid being seen as the primary source of uncomfortable police and crime stories. He was usually behind them all though, with a succession of explosive exposés of police corruption and he deflected criticism away from himself and his sources by having stories he largely authored run under other reporters' by-lines.

He had engineered a tight network of valuable police informants over the years and he had to protect them all. Even a single corrupt homicide detective could help him with at least 20 homicides a year so he could not afford to jeopardise any of his sources. Police could be ruinously unforgiving if one of their own was exposed publicly as an informant or a Benedict Arnold to the police cause. Retribution would be swift, in a relatively compact city like New Orleans.

These methods worked for him but it took a certain amount of astute stage management. He judged that some stories were just too upsetting for the police hierarchy so it must not be seen where his information was coming from. Most police in a tight environment like a police department got to know who was talking to whom. If they saw too many damning stories under his by-line, they could work out roughly where the leaks were coming from, then Philbin could expect to see his sources drying up. But if the stories were under other reporters' by-lines, they were not so sure. And this fudging was enough to stop most of the witch hunts that generally accompanied his embarrassing disclosures.

He said most police could work out where the leaks were coming from anyway, but they probably figured that if there was no-one clearly to blame they would accept it. And if police felt sympathetically towards Philbin he could manage to keep it all going and his sources kept on feeding him. He was treading a fine line in a way that prevented police from taking any systematic action against him or his informants.

At the same time, he was meticulously careful that his fellow reporters got their facts right and had the right angles. This meant the newspaper retained the clarity and understanding, which only comes from years of patiently chipping away at the police culture. When the damning police exposures hit the paper, as they usually did, Philbin and his contacts were at a comfortable distance from the action and so he retained his effectiveness. Other reporters appreciated the opportunities to break the big stories about New Orleans' crooked cops, "Those are the moments you live for – more than awards – and when everything's hitting on all cylinders you know you're in the zone."

Philbin said there was no newspaper agenda to trip up police or trick them but police always suspected it anyway. Many refused point-blank to divulge uncomfortable facts behind stories and police methods, believing this refusal would somehow make the stories better or more positive. Indeed, refusal to cooperate almost always made stories more sinister. The police bureaucracy took critical stories personally unlike politicians or other prominent people who became skilful players in the news process.

Sometimes it was the fault of amateurish and self-serving police public relations. He said he no longer trusted police public relations in his own city because he reckoned he had been lied to so often. Selective operational police had been warned not to talk to him and police made a full-time job of not having anybody in the department talk to the press. They often overlooked the fact that a reporter could simply be driving to get to the bottom of stories and to find out the truth.

Joey Ledford, Atlanta

Joey Ledford said getting too close to police sources was a familiar dilemma for newspaper crime writers. There were many pressures on editors to be more aggressive with crime reporting, but reporters needed to stay close enough to get information without becoming too involved or too sympathetic to police views. But one reporter (no longer with the paper) had such an 'in bed' relationship with police that he sold his car and used to get rides to work in police patrol cars. Squad cars picked him up at home and drove him to the edge of the police district, where he was collected by police from the next district and so on until he got to work.

"It got him a lot of stories but there were questions of police corruption and we had to ask the question, because he got so tight with the cops."

Ledford said the newspaper had overcome jealousy and rivalries between police reporters by introducing a 'cluster system'. Around 15 reporters were covering police and crime and working to line editors and paired off or put into teams. That way the newspaper could take a 'holistic' view of crime news and treat all crime with city-wide importance. Often a regional crime news story led Metro editions city-wide. It made the paper more attuned to crime news trends and made stories more relevant to the whole community instead of just part of it. Line editors were involved directly in all stages of producing stories from conception to meeting deadlines and reading and editing copy before it went to copy editors. But was this crime reporting by committee? It seemed to lose the richness and understanding of having close relations with serving police.

Ledford said the high point of 300 homicides in 1979 had been Atlanta's 'bad year' with the worst crime news figures per capita in America and possibly the world. But crime no longer dominated newspapers anyway. Reporters were asked to put stories into perspective and show how important or relevant they were.

Crime on television was far scarier than newspaper coverage, which aggressively marketed crime news based on the 'If it Bleeds it Leads' approach. Ten minutes of all television news broadcasts were devoted to 'who got shot, who got raped, who got robbed'. It was not uncommon for the lead TV story to amount to little more than a graphic crime news brief. But crime news still had to be big or different to be used on the front pages of the *Journal-Constitution*.

* Joey Ledford was on the *Journal-Constitution* for more than 20 years before joining United Press International for eight years. He wrote *Speed Trap, and Elkmont*: *The Smoky Mountain Massacre* set in Tennessee in 1970.

Al Larkin, Boston

Al Larkin started on the *Boston Globe* as a young police reporter in 1968 when all newspapers had reporters working from permanent offices in the Boston Police Station. Such proximity to police was profitable and reasonable then and they were all told of breaking crime events. This meant they could get out to take photographs and obtain rich context and explanations from police and witnesses. It delivered all the drama and immediacy.

Looking back, Larkin said relations with police had been too cosy and friendly, but the opposite was now the case. Police and journalists seemed to have become adversaries and homicides no longer commanded a high profile in newspapers or in the wider community. Other editors and newspaper executives were expressing the same lingering doubts about being too close to the police.

Larkin said that in the early 1970s Boston's homicide rate had been far worse with more than 100 people killed each year. Murder attracted a lot more attention then – and if a convenience store clerk was shot and killed it would almost certainly be reported on page 1. Mostly though they were a result of hold-ups or gangsters shooting each other.

Homicides were still being given prominent news coverage in 1995 and the *Boston Globe* was still chasing crime stories aggressively. But Larkin pointed to a news report about a shooting death overnight involving a 17-year-old youth, who had been shot in the back of the head just around the corner from his home. The story did not make page 1 and it was not even on the front of the Metro section, instead it was a minor report on the inside pages. The shooting had happened at 5 pm leaving the newspaper plenty of time to gather details:

This is a commentary on what we think [of reporting homicides] today. The randomness of violence makes us take it for granted sometimes. In those days, although there were more homicides, they didn't have the same randomness. They were more explainable and predictable. It's a terrible commentary when a 17-year-old kid is shot to death and it becomes matter-of-fact news. It's not a perfect example but he was only 17.

Larkin said one explanation could be that police and journalists themselves were not as affected by the crimes involving others in the community. But there was a body of people who crime did affect, in particular those out of work who could expect to be shot any day they left home. "Whether they are police, politicians or journalists the fact is that more of them aren't victims and there is not a huge awareness of having to deal with it."

John O'Brien, Chicago

Senior figures in major newspapers and police agencies tend to develop mature long-lasting ties as they get older and move into more responsible jobs. The reporters usually maintain their connections as the years pass and in this way much of the institutional rivalry is nullified. It builds a strong level of interaction that stays off the news pages. But it informs debate and helps to provide newspapers with a better understanding of law enforcement issues.

John O'Brien was such a veteran, a proven and established police reporter at the *Chicago Tribune*. He had already spent 35 of his 37 years in journalism on the crime round and his role now was fleshing out the broader issues of national importance and staying in touch with police at the top. He was a specialist in organised crime, police and investigations of government, the Cook County courts and criminal justice systems.

He joined the *Chicago Tribune* in 1962 and was a walking omnibus of Chicago crime and police from the days before drugs and handguns became bywords for modern violent crime. He still relied on the crime reporter's handbook, which was based on mutual trust. O'Brien said he would routinely call up his police contacts to discuss many non-crime news issues simply because they tended to know so much.

O'Brien did not cross some undefined boundary between impartiality and closeness. He was a skilled police reporter from the old school who had perfected his own brand of crime coverage. In one instance O'Brien arrested a probation officer in the act of taking a bribe. He had been tear-gassed and overcome by noxious leaking fumes while covering stories and he was stoned by a street mob after the assassination of Martin Luther King.

Police were invaluable informants because they had 'big ears on lots of happenings' and they had useful insights into politics and changes on the police scene. "I like to bounce things off them. They have got great minds."

He said police in Chicago were seeking new ways to cut through barriers and to get police closer to the streets. He was interested in a local Child and Parenting (CAPS) program introduced in 1994 by Police Chief Rodriguez. CAPS brought police closer to the community by putting the public on a client basis. It took a much greater interest in communities rather than driving through in patrol cars with the windows up. CAPS cut across all city agencies, including health and urban services, and it gave police a much stronger say in local affairs by giving them the clout to get things done. District commanders told him they were hiring civilian administrators for their respective divisions to get rid of the paperwork and allow more time to meet with community groups.

As a result, police were being greeted more warmly in communities where crime was high. This in turn made them more effective in gaining intelligence.

O'Brien has held many roles across the criminal justice system in Chicago. He was chairman of the Chicago Press Veterans Association, which awarded scholarships to aspiring new reporters. He shared the 1982 *Chicago Tribune*'s

Edward Scott Beck Award for uncovering details of a federal investigation into Chicago's commodities markets. He was also awarded the American Bar Association's Silver Gavel Award for exposing widespread cronyism in selection of local judges and delays to criminal trials, and he earned United Press International's outstanding achievement award for reports on Tylenol poisoning.

* O'Brien has written five books on crime: *Polish Robbin' Hoods*; *Teresita, Voice from the Grave*; *Murder Next Door*; *Getting Away with Murder*; and *Chicago Heist*, a story about Chicago's biggest robbery.

The Scotsman

The Scotsman was one of few newspapers that did not have a dedicated police reporter and crime coverage was usually assigned by the news desk or covered by duty reporters. General reporting staff would make frequent calls to the police media office to see what was happening because police scanners were illegal in Scotland. Having no police or crime reporter or being blocked from using radio scanners usually amounted to poor police-newspaper relations and low crime coverage. And this is exactly how it was.

But in Edinburgh all sides had resigned themselves to doing the best they could in difficult circumstances. Since serious crimes were so infrequent anyway it made more sense for the news desk to assign a reporter for breaking crime. But it also meant little effort was going into building closer ties with police or gaining a better understanding of working together.

Newspaper reporters in Edinburgh said crime coverage suffered because strict judicial guidelines hampered the release of information about police investigations. Senior reporters were assigned to cover breaking national police or crime stories and they would pursue links with the higher levels of the Lothian and Borders Police. But newspaper-police relations were patchy and unproductive with blame on both sides. The lack of any established access to individual police prevented any closeness from developing.

Chapter 16
Behind the Blue Code

Crime and police reporters somehow always managed to fill a growing void in newspaper news lists by retaining their longstanding friendships with police informants. They were artisan journalists who dug out crime stories every day from inside a military-style police machine. The story of crime reporting is one of the untold sagas of modern journalism, about pathfinders on a strange human frontier. They would trail police out to places where life and death were a familiar scenario, where every night would bring stirring new adventures or dangers. They would have to shrug off antagonism and prejudice from some in their own newsrooms.

As society changed and police fell out of favour, newspapers began to draw back from police. They would lose the richness, potential, diversity and advantages offered through access to the inner police culture. The senior editorial hierarchy began to look down on police stories by their own crime reporters with cynicism, and crime as irrelevant, biased or trivial. They disregarded the great sweep of police work and their overarching role at the centre of society, crime, justice and the law. This was a breakdown that was to have heavy consequences for both sides. Police would become more isolated and inward looking and newspapers would find it much more difficult to cover breaking crime. This led unavoidably to a state that exists today where crime and violence are rarely given any context other than the most basic mention. And an undeclared feud has gradually overwhelmed the former view of the world they once shared.

Masterful, well-researched newspaper articles in the mid-1990s still showed the best of crime investigative journalism, writing talent and insight. But many anti-police campaigns proved to be opportunistic, flawed or shallow. Often, they showed a deep-seated lack of faith in police life. Some writers had never seen the troubled and difficult police lives. They ignored the self-sacrifice and courage or how tragedy and violence defined their days and nights. They had not served an apprenticeship on the police round and did not have the right to sit in judgement on them.

But the greatest loss is the access to city life, which police know more about than anyone else. Police give a city its corporate memory and they form lifelong attachments with all the prominent citizens and leaders in politics and industry. They develop a comprehensive body of awareness of the history and are usually highly regarded for the work they do in assuaging grief and tragedy and in adding their weight to efforts to improve the lot of the poor and disadvantaged. In short, newspapers lost the best friend they could possibly have. And in turn the rest of the media have suffered because newspapers were always the first to dig out complex or breaking news and giving it context, explanations and recognition.

Crime is Widely Underreported

There are very few good corporate reasons why newspapers should write about crime and police investigations at all. It represents an on-going drain on resources and the subject matter often raises public discomfort and it could get newspapers in trouble with the courts. These are among the many economic, social and judicial reasons why newspapers should avoid reporting crime. And this appears to be where newspapers have ended up. The decline in newspaper interest in covering crime seems to be global and it is even more complex.

Crime is omniscient, it is everywhere in society. But crime does not translate into public awareness if it is not explained through the media, and I found this to be a failing of newspapers everywhere. Crime is widely underreported by newspapers and the media in general in America, the UK and many other western countries.

America was experiencing an undeclared national homicide crisis and it was not just measured in the number of deaths, although this was bad enough. Vast areas of American cities are among the most impoverished and violent in the modern world. Crime reporting was once the most central city round for any newspaper and a vital connection to the realities of society. But this type of reality on a daily basis does not send out the right messages to a mainly middle-class readership. The same is true for advertisers. So even during the upheavals of the early to mid-1990s, newspapers were more interested in appealing to readers than giving an honest appraisal of life in their own cities. This began to rule police out of the equation.

Newspapers are highly attuned to exploiting big events – the death of a president or a Gulf War. Then the front pages flare into life with graphic photographs and bold headlines when page1 layouts are treated with sumptuous skill. This emphasis on prominence is a feature of newspaper page design where one story of the day must be considered the winner and chosen as the front-page lead. Most days though, stories chosen to lead newspapers are simply the best of what is around. Something has to lead the paper and a choice must be made from the stories at hand.

On quiet days editors begin to look more closely at peripheral crime events to fill gaps in the news pages. Even so, news teams generally prefer not to reflect the nuances of violent crime unless the event is big enough or they are having a bad news day. The infrequency of page 1 crime coverage reflects many things about the structure and focus of newspapers and their long and troubled partnership with police. This does not mean that violent crime is uncommon, it is just one implicit message newspapers fail to deliver.

Indifference

But by the 1990s most newspapers were tiring of a single-victim monoculture, such as one more Ramos Kid shot down in the San Antonio projects, one more forgotten bloodstain along the Cocaine Trail. Much of this is due to the frequency and the endless succession of such killings and subsequent sorrow and hand wringing. Editorial staff would ask each other how anyone can find new and interesting ways to keep on saying the same thing day after day, year after year? It reflects an over-familiarity with serious crime bordering on contempt. Newspaper methods followed the same selection pattern everywhere as news teams sorted through a universe of stories to find usable issues and events. Only a fraction of homicides and shootings took place in circumstances that lent themselves to headlines or eloquent elegies in editorials. Most homicide victims got a few dry words in an obituary column if that.

An important outcome of this lack of genuine interest comes from the way police have been squeezed out. They were side-lined from shaping stories, giving tipoffs and ghost writing most of the crime stories, which meant some details could deliberately be left out as part of this payoff. Editors knew their main task was to produce a paper every day using all means at their disposal. Frequency also affected turning crime stories into glib one-liners, which hid from view the real extent of the killings. It was a side of America no-one wanted to talk about.

The newspaper industry has inadvertently created its own version of reality not the one that exists on brutal streets in dangerous suburbs. People live there under different rules alongside a brooding subculture of drug-related threat, omniscient gangs and saturation gun ownership.

In the not-too-distant future police/crime reporters, the greatest source of crime coverage they ever had, would be abandoned into the wastebasket of history. Newspapers were soon to follow.

The Blue Code

All these setbacks drew police together and strengthened the blue code, which is resentful and suspicious of outsiders but incredibly loyal to those on the inside. A true police roundsman would try to enter this rarefied air and become a part of the police world. From here, the best reporters become vantage points for deeper truths and events drawn from city life. It can be a precious and fleeting state that symbolises the best of ethics and honesty. But getting there can only be achieved by truth and unshakeable fairness.

Losing connections to this inner world of policing comes at a cost. The biggest, darkest anti-police story in decades, the OJ Simpson investigation, was derailed because of the poor relations between the *Los Angeles Times* and the Los Angeles Police Department. The trial was hijacked instead by television, just like the Rodney King case before it.

One after another, these tough-talking, mild tempered individualists told me of their secretive existence as they wheedled and coveted hard-won trust relationships with street-savvy police and detectives. Crime reporters formed the backbone of newspaper crime coverage in cities everywhere. In their networking and journeys of exploration of crime news from the 'inside', they set an atmospheric standard of journalism. They penetrated the opaque police culture and were a perennial part of the crime scene and the general backdrop of life in every city, and it as the police who made this possible.

Some excelled and continued producing wonderful news copy by retaining their networks of informants. Others fell by the wayside, unable to plumb the depths of their own character to truly be a police/crime reporter. Some were poor imitations, relying on media handouts or using the police round as a springboard to accuse police departments of corruption for the sake of a few by-line stories. A skilled crime reporter always found ways to get the messages out without undermining his (or her) mutual connections with police.

They generally did not leave the police round by choice and suffered the suspicion of editors and other journalists, who misunderstood the challenges and skills of crime reporting.

A few failed miserably because they were temperamentally unsuited to the work. They had no passion for the difficult police lifestyle or the lurid crime that dominated life in the ghetto. They could not forge the same depth of trust-based relationships or get the same stories from police informants.

Some crime/police individualists were targeted by newsroom politics or envy – the crime round is very glamorous and desirable for recent arrivals on the news desk, seeking to make a name for themselves. Increasingly, crime stories were being spiked or cut to fill a gap in a page, simplified into acceptable stereotypes or held over to become old news. Often, newspapers began dropping crime coverage without informing their readers. Nor did they want to be seen as an arm of the police public relations effort. This latter pitfall is a genuine one that most reporters and editors watch for.

Crime and police reporters told me of their admiration for police, or in some cases and in some cities their dislike. The police-newspaper connection was a fickle one, which varied from a solid sense of teamwork in San Antonio to the distrust of Los Angeles. In some places though these two fundamental institutions were distracted by their own undeclared cold war.

Newspapers once wrote about the hidden lives of police, the changes in the police hierarchy and carefully reporting police efforts to win salary increases and better working conditions. But these had begun to be seen as 'soft' stories that were forced to compete with other types of news. This neglect of the police lives damaged the standing of the same reporters who were trying to build trust and a reputation for being sympathetic to the police cause. There are ways newspapers and police could work more profitably together. They could run weekly police blotters to reveal what is going on and where crimes are taking place that affect ordinary families, such as the locations of burglaries, robbery or car theft. But interest in police blotters – as with all soft police stories – was disappearing well before I left newspapers in 2003. This was part of an overall fragmentation and dumbing down of newspapers in an effort to survive the financial crisis brought about by competition from the internet, websites, on-line news, bloggers and social media. It makes an important point though, that newspapers are becoming more and more irrelevant.

Chapter 17
Fallen Angels

Police and newspapers once enjoyed a lingering and undeclared companionship, which lasted for decades. But this old friendship was eroded away by time and changing social values, mistrust and dislike. Newspapers had become part of Noel Chomsky's 'military-industrial-political machine', the rank source of money and power. They had evolved into massive international publishing hegemonies focussed wholly on advertising revenue and assembly-line news production. This in turn created media empires for news barons, like William Randolph Hearst or Rupert Murdoch, the head of the News Corp empire. The profession of journalism became the embodiment of the Free Press and Voice of Democracy. But drastic changes in social values substantially undermined these aspirations. Fearless news gathering has given way to the survival of the newspaper corporate entity vested in advertising. This is why it makes more sense to seek out trivia and whimsy because they appeal to readers and make newspapers readable, interesting, eye-catching and buyable.

Police have little in common with news that is really just light entertainment. Anyway, newspapers now have their focus on survival and recapturing lost advertising revenue. Any closeness with the fallen angels of the police is the last thing on their mind.

Clashing Cultures

Newspapers were unprepared and unable by their own philosophy to tell the story of police life – in terms other than the same drama that drives Hollywood and television to glorify violence. Putting a homicide into a 'news brief' meant they had fulfilled their obligation to record the event. Beyond that, there was little genuine interest in broadening coverage of crime and by extension telling the story of the difficult lives of police. It is largely thanks to a collapse of support by newspapers that police are widely seen as fallen angels.

Another explanation for the loss of faith between police and newspapers is the clash of contrasting cultures. The points where they interact are blurred and police, newspapers and reporters all conspire to protect their own best interests. Police want to retain operational integrity and enhance their reputation; reporters want to break down the barriers; newspapers want access to police operations, none of which are free. Police once enlisted newspapers to sanctify the existing order and their role in the defence of it. Instead, both organisations vie for control of the crime narrative.

Violence and crime have little capacity to shock those most directly involved with spreading the news, newspaper city desks, editors, reporters and law enforcement agencies, as well as political, media and corporate propagandists. The chaotic portrait of city life does not radiate outward as a single clear message through the pages of newspapers. Crime and social collapse across the forgotten inner cities do not enter the psyche as one of the great issues now facing modern society on a global scale.

Uniqueness

Newspapers that once routinely covered homicides had begun sorting through them for the more different or captivating, rather than important, because this was the evolving philosophy of news. The police role behind the scenes was rarely explained anyway, so police easily loomed as wooden stereotyped figures who carried guns as society's ultimate raw authority. Routine police activities were not judged newsworthy, but their misdeeds were, and these soon gained disproportionate weight and were widely reported.

This relentless imbalance conveyed to readers a distorted picture of police and what they did. The erosion of the police image has taken decades. It is highly unlikely there was a sudden disintegration of police moral values everywhere at the same time. It cannot be attributed only to live-time television, although this has replaced much of the former police mythology with graphic visual reality. Decades of dealing with the same police department through hard times and good meant nothing to newspapers. Police are bewildered by this because they believe in a handshake and simple truths and trust. Their job makes them this way. They spend their days and nights exposed to human frailty and so often drawn into whirlpools of awful tragedies and cold-blooded crime.

But few police departments have moved with the times either. Their media policies are naive and insulated from real life. In cities like Edinburgh, Manchester and New Orleans the police press office was usually the last to know anything, and they were unable to provide any sustained dialogue with newspapers. Instead, they would prepare press releases saying they had little or no information to offer. Over decades this has added to a deep mistrust of police motives, and it is little wonder that newspaper reporters were avoiding the police media if they could.

Newspapers traditionally conveyed something of the morality of the wider police culture and its rituals, more so than television. They would run 'soft' stories as a trade-off for getting help with breaking crimes. But there was very little serious effort by newspapers to portray the importance of police to a free society any more than police public affairs units could.

Police have a range of responsibilities that go beyond simply collaring offenders and sending them to prison. Clearly, if police charged all who came before them then the jails would be even more overcrowded and the courts overwhelmed. Live TV or radio broadcasts rarely show the hidden depths of police work in a diverse and evolving society, their long shifts punctuated by brief flurries of action where they are not always the central actors. They spend hours on traffic detail, or work night shifts, become embroiled in unpredictable calls over domestic violence, clear the streets of drunks or record details of road deaths, suicides and homicides. No-one writes about how police officers must explain the loss of a child to a grieving parent.

Erosion of Faith

Newspaper articles focusing on police misdeeds mirrored the disintegration of their long collaboration. But it also pointed to a fundamental collapse of acceptance that police were living symbols of the law and should be given respect. It was evidence of the withdrawal of support by an old ally, a blunt refusal of newspapers to peddle police views and propaganda and a new mood that newspapers should not be an arm of the police department. Corporate newspapers in league with big money did not see the police world as fundamental to their own needs. Each individual police officer was still regarded by many as a symbol of the rule of law but sadly this has changed.

What do laws and policing mean in 2023 for a society evidently so massively fragmented? Whose social order do police uphold and protect? Where are the limits to official power or to the type of enforcement police use in a society where morality, violence, weapons, drugs, jail, racism, poverty, freedom and coercion have become blurred concepts?

These questions go deeply to the heart of law enforcement and shape the way the public perceives what police do and how they do it. Yet police still cling to the redundant idea that they are the embodiment of social order and that is how they doggedly expect newspapers to portray them. Instead, they appear in headlines as racist, bigoted, corrupt and violent.

But what's worse, they have no idea what to do about it.

Police were called to a shooting on the west side late last night involving local gangs. Police said they found two bodies. They have appealed for witnesses.

This vacuous crime brief could now be a standard homicide report in any metropolitan newspaper today and yet the police involvement is shown to form the basis of the story. That is because police are the primary authority that all media can quote and attribute the facts to. The peculiar demands of news, to be brief, to focus on novelty, to search for the unusual, to promote angles, means this is how police are: wooden and without any real feelings and there solely to make stories credible.

No-one is Listening

Inner-city crime zones are unexplained mysteries which for most middle-class newspaper readers belong to fiction or provoke disbelief. Most Americans who drive a family car and consider themselves to be at least middle class do not risk driving through these streets and reporters only go there when they have to. One more casual, anonymous, featureless tragedy is not a news event and leaves no indelible imprint on anyone's memory. There was at least one homicide and many shootings every day in each city I went to. But such is the legacy of decades of brutality and the widespread use of guns that no one is listening anymore or feels such things are unusual or even newsworthy.

The news content in metropolitan newspapers is easily shrouded in symbolism and mythology and so is the largely invisible backdrop to urban crime. Newspapers prefer to give out messages that their cities are dynamic and shot through with hope, civic pride, economic promise and a future. They endlessly caricature well-known public figures like sports heroes or celebrities in adulated phrases because it is the easiest job on the paper to rewrite a news release. Or they can tear down the imagery as they so often do if they uncover a breath of scandal or corruption.

The rise and fall of so many is a regular theme for newspapers for they do this job so well. It conforms to the role newspapers carve out for themselves and identifiable personalities and events are visible, easy and interesting targets.

But rarely do they portray the dreadful alternative reality of crime and poverty in the projects facing the hard-pressed dress-blue police line. Residents in this largely forgotten corner of society live every moment in fear of guns and drugs, which have turned inner cities into battlegrounds. No one wants to read about that every day and why should newspapers force them to when they are only there to make a profit. Papers strive to suit consumer tastes and they are well read and respectable. Why should they put that on the line?

Brushing Crime Under the Carpet

This is axiomatic to my argument that crime as a news subject is rarely put on display. The reasons for this are awesomely complex and lost in the blurred mystery of newspaper production, media ownership, modern city living and attitudes to crime, poverty and minorities. Crime is reported along a continuum from very little or nothing at all – or on rare occasions to thundering front page sensations. There are many reasons behind this imbalance.

News professionals admit they cannot provide worthwhile explanations for the extent of crime regardless of how horrific it is. This erodes their willingness to report what they don't understand, and yet they say readers are unlikely to be moved by them anyway. The logical conclusion to this is that crime is just not news anymore by some unspoken consensus.

There is no denying that police and newspapers have drifted apart. The traditional newspaper police reporter with his working-class ethics and innate respect for police symbolism have fallen on hard times. College educated reporters have little truck with the give and take handshake mentality of police, whose careers are built on the rock of hard experience. A generation of police reporters has evaporated in many big cities almost overnight, to be replaced by crime desks and young reporters learning the ropes. Police have been abandoned by their one-time allies.

Police Forgotten

The dangers and risks inherent in a military-style police life are rarely talked about anymore. Once, newspapers would devote time and space to allow their police informants to speak about their inner turmoil. But those days are gone, along with the rich diversity of old-style police coverage.

Police still go out on shifts into dangerous, decaying, unlit inner cities, facing saturation gun ownership, street gangs, drug use, poverty and inequality, broken families, degraded housing and sadistic cruelty. Problems out on the streets are not solved by police, who are outsiders, but at the point of a gun. America did not invest in rebuilding the decaying inner cities – but it did go through a national buying spree to build more prisons and more theme parks.

It should be news when someone is gunned down on the streets by a teenager for a jacket or a few dollars. But it isn't, and no-one could convincingly explain why. It was 'just the way things were' in the inner cities. Widespread anti-police, anti-crime rhetoric was embedded in newspapers across America and in the UK. But police do not help themselves by refusing to cooperate with news outlets. In my opinion this is the greatest failing of all. It would not hurt police to prepare an overview of a crime event that has enough facts to be run as a story then hand it out at a news conference or on-line without infringing the rights of suspects. This would give police control of the public narrative.

Newspapers only need sufficient facts and context to run a crime story. It's not too much to ask and it would take maybe 30 minutes to write. A breaking story can be told in four or five paragraphs. A page lead need only be 500 words. The anonymous police informants who once provided all the big breaking crime stories are now a dying breed as well but so is newspaper interest in writing about it anymore. And this is a tragedy for any national understanding of police lives or the crime environment.

America's homicide detectives are forced to treat each new day and each new corpse as a routine, which they endure in silence and are unable to explain the toll this takes on them. They tackle these frightful jobs without fanfare or expressing too much emotion, often far more interested in not being unfairly caricatured in a media sideshow.

Crime no Longer News

By the mid-1990s, a single homicide was usually not page 1 news unless it was a slow news day or unless reporters could get information from police media before deadline. Such coverage as America had enjoyed down the decades relied almost entirely on anonymous police from the scene.

Most newspapers showed interest in occasional double or triple homicides but not soft stories on crime trends, the plight of victims, state of the inner cities etc, and very rarely – if at all – about police life. Editors shied away from nightly homicides, armed robberies or drive-by shootings that did not involve a killing. Each one meant a lot of effort for very little news copy, perhaps a brief on an inside page if they were lucky but without context or explanation. Killings must have some additional, unusual or unique angle to qualify, and offenders and their victims must be out of the ordinary, either very young children, sports personalities, public figures, celebrities or politicians.

White offenders and their victims usually get coverage, often reflecting the ethnic and cultural make-up of editors in news conferences. Even then, such titbits of crime compete with myriad other news topics and local, state, national and international news. But if nothing else, most newspapers in America do put out an annual omnibus edition on annual crime statistics. First, it is handed to them already assembled by the police. And second, they can run them on a slow news day when nothing else is going on. No-one bothers about crime statistics in the UK.

Selective newspaper crime coverage gives the illusion that crime is under control when it is as bad as ever.

Race Bias

Newspapers and police must share the blame for a breakdown in reporting violent crime. In October 1994, Mark Fitzgerald (from *Editor & Publisher*) reported about Los Angeles Police Chief Willie Williams telling a Unity '94 Conference (for minority journalists) that he knew in advance how the media would treat crime. He wished reporters would pay more attention across the board:

If the victim is a white male or female – particularly if he or she is elderly or, in recent years, if the victim is a foreigner – special attention will be paid [by the press]. If we could get 10 per cent of the publicity we get in some crimes [paid to] other murders, we could solve those crimes. Because someone knows what happened in those murders.

A more typical press reaction is to highlight some crimes and completely ignore others. When two Japanese exchange students were killed in a Los Angeles carjacking it quickly became an international story. "No-one asked about what happened to the other seven murders that occurred that day," Chief Williams said.

Washington Post reporter Nathan McCall told the same conference that when he was a police reporter in Atlanta he would review upcoming stories with his editor. Almost inevitably coverage differed depending on whether the crime victim lived in the predominantly black south side of the city or in the predominantly white north side.

"If it happened on the south side he would say, 'Give me a brief." And if it happened in the north he would say, "Let's look into that one." McCall, the author of *Makes Me Wanna Holler: A Young Black Man in America*, said the implication was that people on the south side were just homicidal blacks who committed murder. When it happened on the north there must be a story in it.

Mark Fitzgerald said some African American journalists believed race-based crime coverage was so systemic it was virtually unconscious. Bruce Johnson, news anchor at *WUSA-TV*, Washington D.C. said, "If there is any sin it's the sin of negligence. It's the fact that there are only white men sitting in that room [for news budget conferences]."

However, Charles Ogletree, chairman of Harvard University's Criminal Justice Institute, disagreed that coverage was just negligent or not intentionally racist. "I think people want to cover crime a certain way," he said. "I think they want to promote images in a certain way. Ninety-nine per cent of black people don't commit crimes and yet we see images of black people day in, day out, and the impression is that they are all committing crimes."

In the Nieman Reports (winter, 1993) Margaret DiCanio wrote that the media shared responsibility for ignoring the soaring toll of violence in the nation. It had been left to the criminal justice system to solve alone. "In its special responsibility to support America's democratic way of life, media coverage of violence has been negligent," she said. "…the media failed to sound the alarm." She said the media had failed to dig beneath the surface to interpret events and omitted stories that needed to be told. "Banal treatment of violence is evident in print headlines and in lead-ins to broadcast news that treat violence like any other story."

Limitations of time and space had been permitted to trivialise violence and make it appear normal. This normalisation of violence by the media and entertainment industry made violence an option to solve a problem. Disagreements between family members, friends and neighbours that might end up in a yelling match now ended with a permanent solution – one contestant dead the other in prison. Daily scores on victims and novel killing methods moved news ever closer to violent entertainment.

DiCanio said coverage of violence in the suburbs and rural areas made class divisions by ignoring the levels of violence outside the inner cities, evident in rape and domestic violence data. "Editors, journalists, and producers now censor non-violent fare because they contend the public has an appetite for violence." She said interpretive stories about violence were scarce. The daily look-alike headlines and look-alike stories had helped to perpetuate a sense of futility and doom. Progress towards a solution for the escalating epidemic was stalled as a notion that violence was inevitable, a notion that the media seldom questioned.

All these ideas pointed to two colliding worlds: one was the real world, the other a belief in what newspapers published. But as I have shown time and again newspapers were crippled in reporting crime and violence, as much by the newspaper system itself as by an acquired sense of news and the judgements of news professionals. But the upshot of all of this is for a gross misunderstanding of urban environments to become the norm and allowed to continue. Violent crime was not being treated as a modern-day crisis that required an urgent cure. It was a state of entropy or of chronic disarray that failed to conform to the clean outlines of news stories and random clever insights or observations. For a single narrative was generally all a big news story could muster. And somewhere along the way, police just dropped out of the picture.

Part Four
Newspapers

Newspapers across the globe were the powerhouses of the media industry in every sense in the glorious years of the 1990s. They had eliminated competition from rival newspapers in most major cities and now they had the greatest editorial workforces in media history. Success was built around outstanding writers, editors and columnists giving unmatched advantages over rival media outfits in radio, TV and cable networks. Crime is given more attention-grabbing treatment on television, but it lacks context and explanations and fails to explain why things are the way they are. This raw footage is the one thing newspapers cannot compete with.

Reporting crime is important in all free societies because it tends to set boundaries, reinforce behavioural norms and makes people aware of what is going on around them. Yet decisions about what to publish or what to ignore are decided by a handful of urban media elites.

Newspapers have been the primary sources of news for hundreds of years, and an essential component of all free democracies. They have always been aligned with law, justice and truth (and the American way). No-one questions their ties to police, who are the primary source of the crime stories that readers trust and which makes clear who the bad guys are. But this quaint idea has disappeared from American life and relations with police agencies were nearing breaking point by the mid-1990s. This one-time amiable collaboration has shifted in all western countries from being cooperative acquaintances to bittersweet and often suspicious adversaries.

But has the future finally caught up with printed newspapers and have they become increasingly obsolete in a virtual internet-driven world that is leaving them far behind? How does crime fit into this picture?

Chapter 18
Newspapers and Crime

Newspapers, so widely feared and respected, have been indispensable to modern society by giving some sense of order to the external world. All newspapers strive to be the same quintessential product each day, because when things are unchanging they radiate stability and predictability. Readers are attuned to this daily routine of sorting through the news and giving it some sort of order.

No-one seriously reads newspapers just for the news anymore. News is just part of the product, and it contributes around 30 to 40 per cent of content. Newspapers are built around advertising; and this is why page layouts have advertising already embedded before the news is superimposed. Maybe traditional readers are looking for the routine of distraction to go with a cup of coffee or as a substitute for a cigarette. Perhaps they have an idea that newspapers contain something from outside their own routine that can make a difference for them.

But newspapers offer something else, something special. They give readers greater context, which usually includes deeper factual content. A newspaper can be read at leisure and it fuels conversations and guides thinking about city life. Newspapers serve to alleviate fear, giving readers a more complete sense of the world than a 30-minute series of nightly crime snapshots on television. News judgments by consensus will decide whether the Ramos Kid who was shot to death in San Antonio is news or not.

Being different and in many senses unique is something editors look for in crime and in news generally. But this is countered by a frustrating subliminal desire to also stay the same and to ensure newspapers are havens of comfort that people can empathise and identify with. Otherwise, it makes people insecure.

Los Angeles Times

Los Angeles Times editors had decided years before not to report individual homicides at all. Capital crimes like homicide and the ensuing shock, tragedy and sorrow were no longer persuasive subjects that met the paper's corporate and financial objectives. And this seems to have been a successful strategy because the *Los Angeles Times* had more advertising content than any other American newspaper by a very large margin.

This was a clear statement about newspaper motivation in failing to report the most devastating homicide rates in history. Metro editor Leo Wolinsky told me there was just too much crime to make any sense of anyway. He said violence short of the city-wide Rodney King riots or earthquakes did not lead the *Los Angeles Times* by any deliberate choice. But the newspaper somehow had to come to terms with a violent city crime rate that was 'staggering' by most other standards:

> It's often not enough to be a brief; there's just so much. There's so much violence and I'm not saying that to say anything special about LA. I think you will see this in a lot of cities, and you don't want to have a paper that simply reflects violence. For instance, if it's a gang shooting to talk about, what sort of societal factors have brought that particular event to bear? Is there a new war under way among gangs? Is there some kind of sociological factor that has gotten these kids into the gangs that have led to this kind of tragedy say with a little deeper meaning? It is not simply a story just of the event.

Wolinsky, who subsequently was appointed executive editor, said it would be misleading to portray street violence and run homicide stories in every edition yet neglect other areas of reader interest. He echoed what I was told in newspapers across America, England and Scotland: it was an anti-crime outlook. It was a nose for something other than crime to fill news pages – and that could mean anything else that qualified as news or entertainment. Editors saw little merit in promoting crime excesses.

This anti-crime bias was even more pronounced where the crime rate was most appalling, like Los Angeles itself, which had around 1,000 homicides a year during the early to mid-1990s. Wolinsky said that wasn't what all life was like in Los Angeles or in California:

We have a limited amount of space [in the news pages] and we want to reflect all the things that go on in the community rather than just that aspect of it. That's because you reach a point I think where it becomes numbing. The question that you pose is whether the readers are getting a true picture of what life is like in LA by reading the paper. Are we misleading them by making it look like there is less violence or are we misleading them by making it look like there is more?

Wolinsky said newspapers were not there just to record events as they happened. They were 'the sorters of facts and affairs' which were put in order in a way that made newspapers meaningful and interesting. This was demonstrated in the way newspapers like the *Los Angeles Times* invested time and energy into studying which stories were the most newsworthy, and how they fitted into some bigger picture of newspaper content. Printed newspapers were 'such personal things' – and most incidents were invisible against a general white noise of crime. Individual shootings, robberies and violence had no inherent power to command news space. Largely because of this approach, very little capital crime was making it onto the front pages of newspapers in western countries.

Atlanta Journal-Constitution

Editor John Walter said newspapers gave comfort and helped to alleviate fear in a form that was manageable – unlike television's style of crime coverage that sent readers 'spinning out of control'. They could be held and read and then re-read at leisure. "You can tuck it under your arm and take it somewhere. You can take your kid to childcare, and it helps you get control of your life. The best of crime journalism is giving someone help and to have a sense of control. Reality tends not to be this way."

The print media helped dispel the mythology of fear of the unknown by presenting the straight facts, raising issues such as a black jurist refusing to vote against a black offender despite obvious guilt. The gulf between 'real life' and the 'reported life' in newspapers produced an impression of city life that had little to do with what was really going on. Or they gave too much space to one and made the readers yawn. But the overriding essence of newspapers was to give people a sense of control over their lives by explaining to them something of the world outside.

Walter said one failing of crime journalism was its inability to find solutions regardless of how dedicated a newspaper was. Crime reporting was always far more than just having a ready source of interesting and provocative stories. It was about being balanced, honest and fair and keeping in mind the nature of the information being put out into the community. The wrong messages could have a serious impact on lifestyle and harmony in a city like Atlanta, which had a marked potential for violence and racial strife. "But saying that the underlying explanations are mostly always absent," he said.

A recent killing by an 11-year-old boy in Atlanta had grabbed headlines because he was the youngest killer in the city to be arrested and charged with murder. Later the same boy was rubbed out by his own gang. News judgments like this had to be made and the public interest was not served by just reporting a succession of the same types of crime. Ultimately public interest went to the question of feeling safe and whether the reader should feel safe and what to do about it. It helped people to come to their own conclusions.

Walter said there was no process whereby newspapers could research these issues and present them to readers with any meaning. This was even more pronounced in Atlanta, a city with very high rates of crime and large areas of poor neighbourhoods. It wasn't that editorial teams like the one in Atlanta were unconcerned about issues such as crime. Crime was simply part of the production process and crime stories were fitted in where they served the purpose of the newspaper in the best way.

No-one Interested

Walter said crime had captured a larger place in society over the previous 20 to 30 years and it still titillated, horrified or shocked readers. Crime splashes raised larger social questions then those questions qualified as news. Newspapers in a metropolitan city like Atlanta must be selective about crime news coverage and not automatically allow 10 inches to every homicide – or for that matter any city story. Walter said some homicides and some violence were often reported out of proportion to other non-crime incidents. "We will divvy up space appropriately. When the bullets fly at the Marta Station it ends up over four columns the next day. When a husband kills his wife in a domestic dispute in the privacy of their own home, it loses public interest."

* John Walter passed in 2008 aged 61.

New Orleans Times-Picayune

Newsroom editor Peter Kovaks was newsroom editor for *The Times-Picayune* in New Orleans – and he said newspapers had to weigh up the news value and prominence given to different types of homicides, such as the sensational death of a police officer compared with a slain drug dealer. Owing to the flow of general news a single homicide on Christmas Day would be afforded more attention than six homicides on a Friday night. This created controversy as people tried to read into news coverage some purpose or reflection of what was going on.

Kovaks said a page 1 story today may only be reported as an incident tomorrow, and people saw significance in news choices that may not have been intended. It would be a mistake for a newspaper to take an attitude of not caring about covering homicides because readers *were* interested. If the newspaper failed to inform readers, they could be disappointed in the completeness of the newspaper. "Imagine if someone was murdered in a neighbourhood and it was heard about by word of mouth or a month later in an association newsletter?"

He needed to be judicious about managing crime coverage because interesting news did not 'just happen' every day. One strategy was to develop a stockpile of 'holdable' local stories that could be plugged in to avoid using wire stories. "Wire stories should never be a default position." He believed mediocre or even poor local news was always better than wire stories.

City editor Colleen McMillar said shootings where victims survived did not make the news pages anymore, except occasionally as briefs and the paper would only cover homicides in any detail when it could obtain timely information. But the New Orleans Police Department did not release much information, and this placed the pressure back on the newspaper to find other sources.

"There is something really sad about that," McMillar said. "Mainly we just try to stay on top. But if we see a trend like muggings in a quarter, we do trend things." Most of the killings were in New Orleans' poorer neighbourhoods where there were 26 in one tiny housing project the year before – yet there was far less danger in more affluent neighbourhoods. "Once the combined income gets above $25,000 homicide rarely touches you."

Manchester Evening News

Editor Michael Unger said an entrenched animosity between newspapers and police was apparent in many societies. He said violent crime was not – and perhaps never had been – a worthy subject for front-page news or even regular news. Unger regarded himself as the one person on the paper who represented the interests of readers, with a duty to give them what they wanted to read. He did this by avoiding a diet of crime on the front-page day-in and day-out. Unger's slant on crime as a legitimate news subject was the same as editors in America had been telling me for months:

> We can't ignore crime, but we do not put it all over page 1. People don't want it – but it is very important that crime is reported.

He pointed out almost as an afterthought that Greater Manchester ranked top in an international study of city property crime and auto theft. Press relations with police in Manchester were poor at best but they were likely to get even worse when police introduced their planned scanner-proof radios. This would put a stop to newspapers monitoring police radio communications. Most newspapers relied on scanners for tip-offs to big crime events as they happened, to get photographers and reporters on the spot. The *Manchester Evening News* was paying a private contractor £150 a month to monitor police radio on a scanner because no-one expected police to tell them when a big robbery or shooting was happening.

Manchester Police Press Office

Richard Flynn said the office in Manchester was poorly set up to handle press inquiries about police operations. Office staff wanted to break the nexus with the news media, but they faced entrenched police attitudes and a dislike for the press that seemed impossible to remove. Much of the office's time and money were heavily invested to help TV networks to produce popular police dramas. This provided a return for police investment by portraying them as more humanised symbols of law and order. It helped explain the role of police in difficult circumstances.

In America some empathy was achieved through informal proximity of police and crime reporters. Flynn said that in practice the average police officer in Manchester was wary and suspicious of news agencies. They were unwilling to speak freely to reporters about the sort of work they did or the operations they were involved in. This came as no surprise to me having found this resentment everywhere. Reporters were forced to try to negotiate deals to get information from a police force that had a dislike of the press and a traditional insularity to public inquiry. Reporters said they were mostly treated imperiously by police who were reluctant to share their secrets and saw them as nuisances.

Crime Loses Interest

The underlying explanations for crime had begun to disappear from newspapers long before the early 1990s. By then, American cities were experiencing open warfare between highly motivated and armed rival street gangs, which controlled large areas of the inner cities. They ran national drug rings and carried drugs up along the Cocaine Trail to every American city.

This time in the mid-1990s was the high point for newspaper dominance of the news cycle too, and the great newsrooms were repositories for the collective corporate knowledge about news production, stretching over hundreds of years. This is where the foundation of journalism is crafted and shaped to reflect the ethics and morality of public life. The newsrooms were also platforms for the accumulated wisdom about police and crime reporting. It was a curious conjunction of newspapers at their most dominant and influential yet a time of the worst homicide rates in history. The irony of all this is that despite all of their dominance, newspapers failed to convey to a national readership the extent of the crisis permeating the inner heart of all major American cities.

The result was to whitewash the true extent of violence and crime from general news coverage. Even shocking crimes were routinely ignored if they did not happen within newspaper deadlines and old news was never given front page treatment anyway.

Ultimately, this was a failing of America's political leadership at a federal and a state level, but essentially the Washington elites who dominate power and money in America. Newspapers have now lost their traditional leadership in covering and explaining crime and the underpinning social malaise that spawned it.

Chapter 19
Mass Produced Entertainment

Newspapers as far afield as Los Angeles, Atlanta, Chicago, Boston and Manchester do not focus on the underpinning urban and social explanations for crime. Media coverage of crime rarely captures the human factor and accounts of homicides appear as fragments that are shallow, trivial, simplistic and stereotyped. Murders should be milestones that reflect a symbolic human reverence for life and death. But newspapers and the media generally have morphed into slick products driving their own social and economic agendas.

Newspapers can only ever be distant echoes of life and death on the streets, and few write with any deeper empathy for the plight of the families of victims in hard-pressed communities. It's the police and emergency workers who are usually on the front lines in obscure and dangerous out-of-the-way places, that everyone else takes pains to avoid. These are usually run-down places with the ever-present threat of car-jackings, drive-by shootings, sniper fire or armed robbery and assault. Newspapers cannot cover it, but then they never could. The highly selective coverage in news choices is only one snapshot into the hidden world of commercial newspapers.

The story of Yummy Sandifer in Chicago serves as an example. The shock value was because he was so young (he was 11 when he died) and already involved in gang-related killings and major theft. When he was killed by his own gang it added another dimension to the story. It was another killing that lasted for a day or two. His murder was exploited by the media because it was different and unusual – but it was not unusual for Chicago. It shouldn't have shocked anyone because it was just one more death; a routine story about how people lived and died on these estates. Even then, the news jolt did not examine the deeper social causes and the underlying tragedy for so many boys like Yummy. The *Chicago Tribune* was a pacesetter in covering crime and exposing the plight of increasingly younger children out on the public housing estates. But the story of Yummy did not lead to any outrage either.

The potential for such events to create banner headlines was limited, and usually undercut by routine news production processes when the commonplace was discarded or downplayed. Newspapers and the rest of the media are not designed to examine and explain deeper human issues, such as street crime, gangs, drugs and entrenched urban and social problems, where the lives of mainly minority residents are inaccessible. And little of it reaches a national audience anyway because metropolitan newspapers focus only on their own cities and states. They rarely examine issues like the state of prisons, the lives of criminals or the underlying defects of the criminal justice system or city services.

Invisible Human Cost

Newspapers had an entrenched attitude that crime happens 'out there' on the streets, and so they were forced one way or another to rely ultimately on police goodwill for their access to urban crime events. And this is only possible through the diligent undercover scheming of crime reporters using skills, social awareness and maturity. This covert partnership was never something that the police pursued. Instead, departments frowned on it because it meant their organisation had been penetrated by a newspaper. These were qualities that not all reporters possessed, and many of them were easily caught up in anti-police rhetoric. This quickly closed off their avenues to reliable police contacts or the chance to establish themselves with other criminal justice agencies.

The chronic failure of newspapers to fully mirror the extent of so much human tragedy and the accompanying cost for society has left them unpopular, distrusted and discredited. Metropolitan newspapers in America, Canada, England and Scotland routinely avoided reporting violence or crime because editorial decision-makers didn't think they were newsworthy.

This was one of my more unexpected findings. But looking at it from a newspaper perspective helps to understand how and why so much of this human tragedy goes unnoticed and unrecorded. There are many reasons for this, involving complex editorial choices, availability of more interesting news, the over-frequency of certain types of crime, reluctance of police to share information, or simply the unwillingness of a newspaper to continue reporting events that no longer surprise anyone. Routine news coverage once included car crashes (where no-one died), shoplifting, burglaries or fights outside a pub, as some rough examples. Now none of them are reported.

Even in 1995 crime events that made it into the news pages had to have some additional element of the sensational about them, something different – a prominent person, a police officer, politician or government official or something that was more noteworthy. Deaths or routine shooting incidents in sub-standard housing estates were routinely disregarded unless there was something special about them. Most news desks had come to accept as normal the violent nature of the drug trade and gangs and violence was always linked to gang territory or run-down housing estates.

Occasional articles would be run after the release of studies by criminologists on popular issues like drug use, statistics of homicides or other serious crimes, or annual crime reports prepared by police agencies. I had done exactly the same in Australia. But I kept my main focus on strengthening access to well-placed sources and to feed fresh police stories into the system every day. As a result, most of the police media conferences I attended were about stories I had already written about and had been published in the paper that same morning.

Homicides in America usually made headline news when they involved multiple victims, prominent men and women or ultra-dramatic events. Class distinction plays a part too, since homicides usually involve drugs, urban gangs and drug turf wars in the projects. These extensively downtrodden and dilapidated areas on the fringes of American consciousness are widely seen as zones of poverty and failure. Thus, residents are the root cause of their own damaged lives, failures, tragedies, broken families and squalid environments. This is a profound failing of a society to ignore the most vulnerable people.

They are to blame for being trapped there and for failing to strive for a better life. It is a clear case of blaming the victim. But it was a fault of society. Reporters in cities as far apart as Los Angeles, New Orleans, Chicago and Atlanta said they could go out on the projects on any night and hear the sound of gunfire. Residents in these areas could identify the make and calibre of a weapon just from the sound.

Editorial decision-makers were reluctant to have any single issue dominate or hijack their news pages. Newspapers wanted to report what was different or new but not events that happened over and over again seven days a week. And it made no difference for anyone anyway?

Crime stories attracted only token interest in a news budget conference unless events were defined or perceived as 'outbreaks' or where they carried a strong secondary message, such as police promoting better home security, new or deadlier drugs or locating persistent offenders. Crime tended to attract wider interest when newspapers were on a crime crusade. But was this really 'taking an interest' when such exposes led to nothing being done about them?

Numerous factors contribute to such insensitivity, where serious crimes are routinely discarded from news coverage or treated as briefs to fill gaps on quiet news days. Local crime in major newspapers is crowded out by many things but it also depends on whatever news is around on any given day. Newspaper executives recognised that readers were turned off by constant 'bad news' from within their own communities. Thus, by many such means the potential news coverage of crime, drugs, death, homicides and gun-related violence drifted deeper into the paper and away from page 1. This gave a factually misleading portrait of city life and the pervasiveness of crime and criminal behaviour in their midst. So all the soft police stories didn't create a lot of sympathy or understanding in the end.

Profit and Loss

Corporate newspapers are driven by a focus on circulation and advertising revenue and editors who want a more fully rounded newspaper, not one dominated by any single issue. They are acutely aware of the price of getting the news mix wrong because they want to appeal to the broader interests of their readership. Thus, newspapers have evolved to become a form of infotainment, preferring to reflect the lives and events of the rich and famous and their private lives, the turmoil of federal and state politics, local issues of transport gridlocks and road smashes, buses that don't work and railways that are derailed, unsafe high-rise developments, police corruption and the latest soaps and sports heroes. This passing parade gives newspapers diversity and lightness that appeals to the broadest possible audience possible. The assault by the ephemera of modern life has whittled down coverage of crime, killings, drugs, violence and poverty, which are all relegated to the briefs column or as cuttings on the newsroom floor.

Yet still the violence seemed to be unstoppable everywhere along the bruising Cocaine Trail. City police departments encountered shootings and killings on the streets by the hour, sometimes by the minute. Morning police patrols found corpses in twos and threes in the inner cities and the police went out armed like front-line troops in a war zone, as they were in Hollywood. Police describe such patrols as Russian roulette.

Fearful residents in large inner-city areas could expect bullets to fly through the thin walls of their shanty homes after dark. Drive-by shootings were commonplace in these estates and they added a new edge of terror to life in the projects. Police on the West and South sides of Chicago would expect to find corpses when day broke. Few of these events were echoed in the bigger metro newspapers but most were not. Newspapers, just like TV news, have trouble explaining them and generally treat them as briefs because most of what they could write has been said already. But what about the human tragedy?

Disinterest

Homicidal murder has lost the essence of news because it happens all the time. Newspaper executives have become numbed by them, and this disinterest continues today as newsrooms become more depleted by the day. A selection of the most bloodthirsty killings might hit the headlines once in a while, but it depends on what other news is around. Many get no mention at all and are quickly forgotten in the news cycle until a new more ominous incident comes along and jolts newsmakers into putting murder back on page 1. Unfortunately, America's homicide rates resemble Olympic competition and only attract newspaper attention when records are broken.

Each day's newspaper is a product put together with entertainment in mind, and every new edition requires a different set of news content. But it tends to be the same type of news that is being recycled and so sameness becomes an important factor in reproducing the same product day after day. But we must not forget that journalism and news management are directed ultimately towards profit and advertising and retaining a mainstream middle-class readership. Many people would believe that newspapers should allocate space to crime and to treat it with some significance. That is the human story that is lost in all this.

The same pervasive news rating process occurs in every newsroom in America, Canada, United Kingdom and Australia. It doesn't seem to matter what the crime is, newspapers are unable or unwilling to report it unless it is a poor news day, or of course unless a major crime incident is just too compelling. Of course, the worst crimes do occasionally get front page treatment but only because they are too big to be ignored.

Circulation and Profit

Many metro reporters and editors are passionately interested in their own cities, but they are not going to allow any single issue to dominate the news pages. Newspapers are there to create a news product, which in turn is the medium for raising advertising dollars. No-one is there to change the world or improve the lives of the humans they coexist with. To them it's just a job.

Reporters from the *Los Angeles Times* to the *Boston Globe* do not pretend to be like T S Eliot, the American poet who wrote about the 'conscience of the streets' in his epic poem *Preludes*. They don't even try to be the conscience for human suffering. Nor do they pretend to have solutions for urban violence or crushing poverty. They are there to report the news and (indirectly) to sell advertising. But changes have come along that have reshaped newspapers into an entertainment product. They are no longer allies of the police or chroniclers of violence as they once were. This has gone largely unnoticed by readers who all buy the paper for the same reasons, to have control over their lives and get some sense of the world around them. Newspapers evolved over many decades to become global commercial entities, where success is measured in the size and scale of circulation and readership, as this table shows:

Daily Circulation

1.	Wall Street Journal	1,854,901
2.	USA Today	1,557,171
3.	New York Times	1,187,950
4.	Los Angeles Times	1,104,651
5.	Detroit News & Free Post	910,707
6.	Washington Post	852,262
7.	New York Daily News	764,230
8.	Newsday	720,352
9.	Chicago Tribune	697,349
10.	San Francisco Chronicle & Examiner	647,373

Sunday Circulation

1.	New York Times	1,767,836
2.	Los Angeles Times	1,502,120
3.	Detroit News-Free Press	1,172,769
4.	Washington Post	1,163,338
5.	Chicago Tribune	1,110,552
6.	New York Daily News	989,721
7.	Philadelphia Inquirer	947,325
8.	Dallas Morning News	841,576
9.	Boston Globe	815,265
10.	Newsday	800,745

* Sources: FAS-FAX, Audit Bureau of Circulation, six months ending March 31, 1994, compiled by the Los Angeles Times.

The battle of the broadsheets is not about explaining the best and worst of human society. It never was. It's about what a small team of editors considers to be the news of the day and what should lead every day is an open question. This pushes editorial thinking into patterns as they try to get this formula right and put all news items into some sort of order. Newspapers are sometimes accused of exploiting crime and tragedy in order to boost sales. This couldn't be further from the truth. Most days crime stories are pushed down the news budget list or fail to register at all. Deciding what leads is a many-sided question with endless dimensions.

This is because the role of newspapers goes far beyond just reporting news. They fill a void in people's lives and become an anchor-point for living. Papers say what is happening and where and readers have come to expect newspapers to fill that gap and to offer ways to quantify their own inner values and hopes. They give people a comfort zone. Newspapers look for drama and sensation but they resist the urge to be running sheets for crime. Violent crime especially is balanced against the relative importance of thousands of other stories competing for a place in the next day's edition.

The under-reporting of crime is lost in a catchy turbulent stream of newsy trivia because newspapers are mass produced entertainment. They are not there to change the world, they are there to make a profit. There is a human dimension to crime reporting, the uneasy tension between newspapers and police departments. This relationship was especially frigid in Los Angeles in the wake of the OJ Simpson trial. Such discord is often more interesting than the news itself. It certainly affects the quality of information shared with newspapers.

The *Boston Globe* news desk was in tune with the police department yet still took the department to court and won over falsified police crime statistics. The *San Antonio Express-News* had the closest relationship I saw anywhere, with a news desk inside San Antonio Police headquarters. This was a rare throwback to the days the Mafia was the biggest story in town. The *Chicago Tribune* had an imposing crime desk with feelers throughout the city to tap into police sources. It was a strongly focussed crime newspaper but even then, it was impossible to report 400 armed robberies or 300 shootings a week. In many cases newspapers simply had no mechanism to report what was going on. There are myriad explanations for it.

By long tradition, newspapers are perceived as objective, impartial and unbiased gatherers of news. But throughout media history American newspapers became increasingly desensitised to undercurrents of violence, which have always has had a place in American life anyway. Vastly higher quantities of deadly drugs are still reshaping society, causing an explosion in drug-related social change. The entire sub-culture of impoverished life across the decaying inner cities is increasingly associated with the worsening drug culture.

So, crime and unequal opportunity *are* connected yet equally regarded with derision and contempt. The frequency of crimes as they sweep through the inner cities creates a sense of disinterest but also of fear. And fear is something newspapers do not want to promote or be associated with. Crimes that were once attention grabbing have become commonplace and news desks began treating homicide, armed robbery or rape with apathy. Somehow the violence has to get much worse to be considered as genuine news.

Most tragedies out on the projects in lower-class neighbourhoods happen in a news vacuum, hidden behind a form of white noise. It's also worth making the point that by long practice newspapers lumped coverage of crime and police onto a single individual. Crime desks were still in their infancy in 1995 as traditional police and crime reporting individualists were being swept away on a tide of change.

Filling an Emptiness in People's Lives

Newspapers have no particular duty to expose the grim underside of city life or lead campaigns for social reform. They are interested solely in news events that will fill news pages on deadline for a single day and there is never time to debate the fine details. News comes in a rush and is dealt with in a hurry, or it doesn't come at all and has to be manufactured. The rules are simple: print and be damned.

Newspapers have become a soporific, a placebo offering comfort and safety. This is what newspapers do, they keep things moving along. They appeal to the inner person and they remind them of their own humanity. They are not there 'to disturb the universe' – as T S Eliot wondered in *The Love Song of J Alfred Prufrock*.

Nor are newspapers anything like the old-fashioned single-issue political pamphlets anymore. They are highly refined products that have morphed into comfort zones that fill an emptiness in people's lives, and they contain a view of society cleansed of its ugliness and fear. Readers tend to breathe more freely when they see things have not changed overnight and some implicit threat is removed from their lives. Meanwhile, out of sight police swap bullets with assailants on Chicago's West Side and gangs rule large sections of impoverished neighbourhoods in Los Angeles.

What to Leave Out

Indifference is a necessary precondition of any newspaper news model, which relies on picking the best news stories and leaving out all the rest. Some issues in society must be routinely overlooked as unnewsworthy, especially if they are commonplace and frequent. There is always limited space for news and great competition in news budget conferences. The selection process is one of the least known skills of newspaper journalism, knowing what to leave out. As W. H. Auden says in his masterpiece, *Musée des Beaux Arts:*

About suffering they were never wrong,
The Old Masters; how well they understood
Its human position; how it takes place
While someone else is eating or opening a window or just walking dully along;

Efforts by police and crime reporters are never enough to break this cycle or tell the unvarnished truth. Few newspapers have a lasting genuine commitment to crusade on issues like crime. Family breakdown, poverty and squalor may be a way of life for many, but frightened residents will look to street gangs for protection instead of the police they fear. In turn the gangs use guns, narcotics and stand-over tactics to enforce their power over people. These images are the ones middle-class newspapers everywhere want to avoid.

Crime is not like other news. It's about human failings that are rooted in our distant genetic past. Crime reporting is as unsavoury for newsmakers on the *The Atlanta Journal-Constitution* as it is for the *Manchester Evening News*. There are always other better and more sanitised news around in a massive global news production machine. It would probably be more accurate to say that newspapers are indifferent to humans rather than indifferent to crime. They keep a watching brief but only report the worst and the best of it.

Justice and Crime Coverage

Crime coverage is often blocked and stifled by uncooperative police or a paralyzing legal system. Property crime rates and auto theft in Manchester are among the worst in Europe but the *Manchester Evening News* does not report much of it. These things are not subjects for regular news coverage and they never have been. They are just frequent and routine background noise that no-one gets to read about. Australian newspapers also treat crime as random unconnected events with no particular rhythm in the news cycle other than slow news days. The worst crimes only emerge somewhere near the top of a news budget conference if and when they have the 'gee whiz' factor.

Newspapers in Australia and the United Kingdom face limits placed on them by sub judice and defamation laws, uncooperative police and restrictive court practices. Editors become ultra-conservative about what they publish because they too face the threats from defamation laws or the courts. Not too many say, 'print and be damned', but some do.

The formal rituals of the justice system versus the right to publish are in place to protect the integrity of investigations and the rights of offenders, which are usually off limits once an arrest is made. Details of names and elements of investigations are treated as sub judice, which means 'before a judge or court of law' or 'under judicial consideration'. These restrictions are very convenient for operational police and detectives, who are reluctant to share their investigations with the news media anyway and are only interested in doing their own jobs and brushing away media inquiries. It's not their job to hand out factual details to the media, their job is to uphold the law.

However, police agencies will not accept any responsibility when a newspaper or other media outlet gets their facts wrong, which happens a lot. Yet this really is a failure of the police and a justice system that seeks to exclude the public's right to know. The irony is that operational police routinely refuse to share investigations with their own public affairs units, who in turn are unable to give reporters enough facts to put a story together – because they can't get them either. Then they have to wrestle with disappointed and anxious reporters, and so a pattern is created. It makes a mockery of the idea of having police public affairs units in the first place if they cannot and will not assist the media.

Finding Ways to Work Together

Editors say they have no mechanisms to report all the crime or all the homicides – because no-one can attach any meaning or understanding to four homicides a day or 30 on a bad weekend, commonplace enough events in Chicago, New Orleans or Los Angeles. Yet the answer seems straightforward to me. Police can easily establish an information channel to write and release all the relevant facts of a case, which means a media outlet has enough details to write a story. This enables police to alert news outlets about what should be left out to protect future investigations and trials. It's a quid pro quo.

I used this approach on numerous police stories where I would go back to my police source to run through the facts. It gives a valuable safety net to make sure I got the story right but also to leave out anything that might prejudice a police investigation or a trial. Usually, such detail has little bearing on a story. One overwhelming benefit is to create a better system for covering breaking crime and strengthening ties between the media and the police. Ultimately, it is the editor who should be making these decisions.

But while this works well in an ideal world, humans in the system just get in the way, as they always do. Choices like this come down to the individuals already in the system, and they all seek to guard and control their own part of it. Trust is rare for such closeness between the news media and police anyway. And that is why the nexus between crime reporters and unnamed police sources was itself the best solution of all.

Chapter 20
Whitewashing Crime

There are many intricate threads explaining how crime has lost its capacity to interest newspapers or jolt readers. I examined this issue with all editors and leading crime reporters across several countries and what I found was confronting and disappointing. Crimes being excluded routinely from news pages included homicides, rapes, armed robberies and violent assaults. They went unreported or were cut down to briefs on news desks because they were not really news anymore. They had become commonplace and familiar and did not qualify as unusual.

Crime stories that were once front-page news were competing with everything else. Unless they could be repackaged or re-explained in some other context, such as involving a police officer, celebrity, politician or a prominent person, then they lost news interest. Editors also expressed concerns about their newspapers only reflecting violence and perhaps adding to a sense of fear or division. They said the role of newspapers was broader than just being single-issue focused, thus driving away readership.

Newspapers do not even try to be mirrors of the societies they report on anymore. Perhaps they never could. What they portray is an editorial reinterpretation of reality each day, a sanitised version of society to their millions of readers. How newspapers cover crime or why (or why not) are among the deeper questions that I sought answers to.

Crime was once one of the most emotive issues in newspapers. A 1980 study with a broad definition of crime news found that 22 to 28 per cent of topics in newspapers were crime-related, 20 per cent of local television news, and 12 to 13 per cent of network television news. The research suggests that American and British newspapers had once overemphasised specific crimes, rather than analyse trends, causes or remedies. The media was accused even then of over-reporting serious crimes, especially homicides, which had consequences for public perception of the police role (cited in 'Media made criminality: The representation of crime in the mass media', Dr Doris Graber).

However, by the 1990s this trend was changing noticeably, and most major newspapers were ignoring crime as a worthy news topic that readers might be interested in. Less emphasis was given to all types of crime, including homicide, burglary, armed robbery, car theft, rape, shooting incidents and violence.

A similar decline in interest was evident for the plight of minorities stuck in the inner-city ghettos. There was a sense that such things were no longer mainstream by newspapers in America, England and Scotland. The *Los Angeles Times* did not report cover homicides at all, despite record-breaking statistics and the *Manchester Evening News* generally shunned any crime. The *Edinburgh Evening News* was prepared to cover crime but faced barriers from uncooperative police and a repressive legal process (at least from a media point of view).

As a general rule, only the worst or most sensational events were getting any headline treatment at all. Serious crimes like homicides were endemic in many American cities but they were mostly downplayed or ignored. A lot depended on ethnicity too. Homicide had become a commonplace event associated with gangs and drugs and the disorder of run-down neighbourhoods. The implications from record violent crime and underlying social causes were rarely connected. Instead, big crime splashes portrayed the worst incidents but without any genuine context or explanations. Almost everything else was whitewashed.

Advertising versus News

News depth has been ground down to a superficial veneer to attract interest in a product that doesn't exist anymore. It's a retail commodity that carries advertising and looks for any convenient selling point. Bad news can be a distraction to this. The real purpose is to justify and encourage market share and advertising potential. Writing about crime or urban decay in plague proportions no longer fits this narrative. Since 2000, newspapers have had far less resources or capability to produce a fully rounded newspaper.

Nevertheless, newspapers still traded on a reputation for being the visible symbols of modern civilization, freedom and democratic thought – most reflect this on their mastheads. Editorial decision-making in daily news budget conferences across the world is not really seeking to sort through real news but to reinforce a way of life or a system of values and beliefs. They are just producing the next day's newspaper as a product that might include news as 40 per cent of the content. The rest is advertising or entertainment.

But at least in English-speaking western democracies there still is an unqualified right to 'ask' questions and to report the news, for what it is. Newspapers traditionally go much further than the electronic media in providing comment and opinion, advocating public policies and furnishing information to readers from different fields of endeavour. This used to be linked to their far broader editorial capacity, larger workforces and capability to explore and report on multiple issues.

But now they produce entertainment and invite readers to collaborate in this deception by publishing their comments through Letters to the Editor.

Such a medium as a newspaper has become an anachronism because anyone with a keyboard can now make public comment on social media. Some keyboard junkies have up to a million or more followers and they wield great influence. Social media has become a new field of pseudo journalism but largely without training or experience and without standards of journalism.

The truth is that no newspaper produces news anymore. Their aim each day is to fill the spaces reserved for news and to sort through all the locally gathered stories and weigh them up against news items from further afield. Locally gathered news was the first to suffer in depth and detail due to a collapse in the size of newsrooms. This has had a profound effect on crime coverage, which is almost universally local in nature. They must appeal to as wide an audience as possible and this means avoiding any single-issue dominance, like crime. This is evident in the way newspapers are broken down into various sections, feature lift-outs, advertising spreads, editorial sections for comment and opinion, sport, metro, editions for zoning, and special features. Space dedicated to news coverage directly reflects advertising volume in every edition and this determines how many pages a newspaper can have.

As readership dwindles, the real measure of success (or survival) is seen only in advertising volume.

Top 10 Newspapers in Total Advertising Volume

Total Advertising Inches – 1993

1.	Los Angeles Times	6,873,562
2.	New York Times	4,596,856
3.	Newark Star-Ledger	4,349,739
4.	Dallas Morning News	3,896,282
5.	Fort Lauderdale Sun Sentinel	3,551,702
6.	Boston Globe	3,422,265
7.	Washington Post	3,110,580
8.	Chicago Tribune	2,939,665
9.	Miami Herald	2,918,815
10.	Orange County Register	

Note: Inches are full-run and part-run, weekday and Sunday combined.

* Source: Competitive Media Reporting.

White Noise

In one sense, newspapers possess the ability to determine what people read about their own cities and the world in general – and what they do not. The editor of *The Atlanta Journal-Constitution*, John Walter, said newspapers had a responsibility to present a balanced viewpoint and not to create divisions or fear. Actual crimes however are manifestly real for victims and their families.

Crime in a modern society is now almost impossible for a newspaper, or any media for that matter, to reflect on in anything other than a very broad sense. Newspaper campaigns rarely led to reforms on any issues anyway, such as sub-standard housing, the rising number of children in the cycle of homicides or highly dangerous housing estates. And no-one should blame newspapers, because it's not their job to drive social reforms or to put in place a vision for better, safer cities.

This leads to the surreal process of small teams of newspaper editors deciding to run crime as a small proportion of much broader overall news choices in order to retain freshness and up-beat moods. In high-crime cities this can only serve to produce an image that has nothing to do with reality. Serious crime reports end up being juggled with many other unrelated stories to find a place somewhere down the news pages. This of course leads to crime stories being cut down to a brief or spiked. Many newspaper executives told me this led to whiting out America's record levels of violence, drugs, killings and shootings.

There was just no shock value in crime anymore, and the real driving force in newsrooms was to complete pages on deadline. But there is something far deeper to all this. Newspaper executives decided that the reading public should not be confronted with reminders of the downtrodden suburbs, persistent killings over drug turf and all the personal grief and anguish this causes. The shootouts and corpses are no longer rare events in most American cities anyway. They are routine and everyday occurrences that all city dwellers are fully familiar with. Collectively, it is the substitution of entertainment for the reality of violent crime and social decay.

Erasing Reality

The ghetto is not a fiction story and nor are the tragedies, unfairness, tears and bullets. These are swallowed up beneath an ocean of other potential news that clamours for attention. What does not make the front-pages are the hidden wastelands where people are dying at the margins of civilisation in decaying housing estates, with armed gangs, dangerous children carrying guns and blue-draped police trying and failing to hold back the tide. Reporters once made fleeting visits to these dangerous neighbourhoods for a few lines of copy to flesh out stories about urban crime or the latest homicide. Snipers sometimes shoot at them.

They were disturbed by what they found and the decaying condition of the houses and infrastructure and the aimless, jobless, homeless and moneyless people they encountered there. But what could they do about it? They don't even write about it anymore. And newspapers can't make sense of it anyway, although many tried.

Newspapers on both sides of the Atlantic were unwilling and unable to provide readers with a regular detailed explanation of the world of crime. They were just as unlikely to cover prisons, courts, police, poor housing, welfare or mental illness, at least not in any depth. Manchester for example had its own extensive suburban slum subculture with gangs, drugs and extraordinary property crime rates, but to the *Manchester Evening News* such things were not news. The environment which was synonymous with crime was little more than a place most people stayed away from.

The treatment of copy by news desks has a decisive impact on how crime ultimately is reported to readers. The news that is gathered must meet special qualifications to be prominently run and must have some angle to make it interesting. News processes mean reports are often thought of, researched and written the same day.

Filling Gaps

Crime must have immediacy to make it into the news pages. News teams must be able to get in, take pictures and hold a few interviews and get out. The story is written in a rush to meet the basic tenets of news: who, why, what, when, where and how. The trouble with crime is that it keeps to no schedule, other than usually occurring late at night or on weekends, when newspapers have only a skeleton reporting staff.

But then news editors and layout technicians must find space on a page that has already been laid out and edited. This space is often a gap, a hole that needs to be plugged. The essence of any crime story is all that stays intact. A trite headline highlights only one aspect of the story, which is cut to length to fit a hole on a page. The remnants of the original hastily prepared report then become a news fragment that focuses on one or two elements of the event. That is called news and it is incredibly misleading.

Mostly, the underlying reasons for downgrading crime are complex and hidden. The decline of news interest cannot be explained only as an obsession with circulation and advertising. It is infinitely more complex than that. Newsmakers want to say to their readers: "Hey, this city is a grand place, a diverse and exciting place. So read me and everything will be okay."

Newspapers and most of the media set out to re-define the news to fit the message. Crime is a reality that most people wish would go away but it keeps hammering home its presence through bullets on the back streets. People are mowed down every night and newspapers simply cannot treat each one as a capital news story.

Neither can they make sense of thousands of armed robberies, rapes, assaults and shootings. This shouldn't mean they don't cover them at all. This incipient failure to portray the urban environment is a defect of the newspaper zeitgeist. Newsmakers say they and their readers have had enough and no longer value crime as automatic front-page news. Crime is not legitimate anymore and this reflects a philosophical inability for newspapers to deal with urban life. News editors ask how they can make murder interesting when they happen every night. Everyday crimes have little news value when there is so much and the few that make it through the minefield are generally big affairs. In such cases, coverage is decided by the television maxim, 'If It Bleeds, It Leads'.

Assembly Line News

But what about the hundreds of thousands of crimes that do not meet newspaper guidelines? Are they forgotten? Did they happen? The crime portrayal is misleading no matter which way you look at it. But is that a failing of newspapers or is it just the way society wants it, a safety valve to avoid inducing too much fear? Newspapers are factories for assembly-line news, advertising and newsprint. An agglomeration of incredibly massive detail must come together to meet deadlines and to furnish an acceptable, saleable product.

This industrial scale process rejects ill-fitting notions of crime and violence if it can, just as it rejects anything that slows down or clogs the system. But despite this failing there is still great romance and drama to be found at the heart of newspapers. It lies in one of the few rounds that touches the pulse of life on the streets, the police round with its glamour and excitement, pitfalls for the unwary, intrigue, drama, sorrow, mystery and sophistication. Yet this touchstone for city life, police and crime is already vanishing from modern life.

The crime stories that do make the news pages are automatically distorted by the very editorial processes that report them. The delivery of crime coverage is stage-managed like all news, depending on how much interest it generates in news budget conferences. They are reinterpretations of occurrences out in run-down estates to create stories people can grasp but which they don't want to see. No individual story can carry explanations about the causes of violent crime, merely to report that they happened. And when there are so many this soon stops being newsworthy as well. The only difference lies in the scale of some particular event. Most people know there are serious urban problems and crime in their inner cities. They just feel uncomfortable reading about them in every edition.

Newspapers are not alone in having a role in unwittingly downplaying reality by ignoring crime. Newsworthiness of crime is also eroded by police forces and other law enforcement agencies that regard the media as a necessary but untrustworthy nuisance and in whom they refuse to confide factual details and explanations. There are many ingredients that go to make up the magic pudding of reality, advertising and fiction. Crime is just one ingredient of the larger whole and an obscure and unimportant one at that.

The giant legendary newspapers seek to recapture their once-great readerships and lost advertising clout. Most were at saturation point for circulation in the 1990s, yet they pushed on hoping to protect or increase market share.

Newspapers are social constructs and news events are an outer façade to a commercial product, like wrapping paper around gifts, with a commercial hard core built on advertising and market share. They are not there to expose unfairness, criminality, unfair living standards or to create reforms, rebuild the inner cities, find jobs for chronically unemployed, right the wrongs and save the planet.

Behind the scenes, newspapers are entirely driven by circulation and ledgers, charts and spirals, which measure success for directors in boardrooms or shareholders on the stock exchange. They are there to sell newspapers and make a profit, the ultimate bottom line. Public awareness of the unpleasant nature of crime is determined by dollars and cents.

Developments in politics and news issues generated by routine presidential statements, overseas violence and turmoil, the economy, sport and civic issues all belong to a quantum that is revisited on a daily basis. Constancy is what newspapers seem to portray best. Yet this creates a paradox where news must be different and the same at the one time. Crime fits very awkwardly into this discord at the centre of newspaper theory.

A predictable pseudo-event where the president signs a memorandum of understanding with a foreign country will qualify as news, because it is a public milestone that should be recorded. A local batch of homicides will not be news for exactly the same reasons. They are not milestones or developments although one might be selected if the victim is prominent or important.

Newspaper news plays a far different role than television news, which is not as personal a product and does not carry a social expectation of value reinforcement. Perhaps this is because people can't buy and possess the news flickering on a television screen in the same intimate way they can take ownership of a printed newspaper. Television is further down the road of visual entertainment and people come to expect television news to be without many of the social mechanisms they expect from newspapers, which they must buy each day.

The messages and meanings that newspapers deliver are recognised by public relations agencies, and they exploit this by presenting their own agendas to fit in with it. Unfortunately, police media agencies interpret these signals very poorly. To make matters worse, the type of crime information they seek to portray inevitably carries underlying coercive symbols. Newspapers portray themselves as the real America, the real thing. But they are not, and cannot be reality. They are just blurred connections between one world and another, a flickering torchlight in the darkness.

Mid-Life Crisis

The declining art of crime reporting by big city newspapers, combined with numerous other factors, signals the end of blood and guts reporting. No-one draws attention to the way newspapers have slipped into a mid-life crisis, where the turbulent problems lying at the core of the inner cities are no longer news and are rarely reported as such.

Editors say almost in chorus, they have an overriding duty for the desirable appearance and content of newspapers. What purpose is there in saying this if it is not for fear of poor acceptance or lost circulation? It cannot possibly be simply about a news gourmet's taste. There is a palpable pressure to be wary about what readers might feel uncomfortable with. It sheds light on the reasons why newspapers are reluctant to treat crime with the same brush strokes as everything else.

This is mirrored by the decline of the traditional police roundsman, the one-time ally of police. There are very few left but they are becoming devalued and non-essential as newspapers drift further away from police and urban news coverage. Some newspapers still take pride in exploring crime as a news event, like a flag run up before a bloody battle. This was true in Chicago, Atlanta and New Orleans but not for Los Angeles or Manchester. Editors as a group seemed palpably unable to recognise that the mechanisms used routinely to collect news contained fatal weaknesses that excluded issues like crime, law and justice.

Groupthink

The concept of the newsworthiness of crime, or of any other disturbing issues, hang on the shared beliefs of generally small cliques of urban newspaper professionals. These choices come from their own personal experiences, which are mostly shared and identical. By the time they have risen to become news decision-makers their opinions are fixed, their backgrounds are almost exclusively from the same environment they preside over, and their ideas are all reinforced by their fellow editors and bureau chiefs.

Such unspoken consensus in decision-making was identified in 1972 by research psychologist Professor Irving Janis, a phenomenon he described as 'groupthink'. This occurs when individual loyalties to a group prevent members from raising controversial or uncomfortable questions. According to groupthink, harmony and consensus become more important than raising difficult moral questions.

A famous example used by Janis is the ill-fated Bay of Pigs invasion of Cuba in 1961. When the decision was taken to go ahead by President Kennedy, his advisers backed it unanimously despite some saying later they had strong private reservations. One of the participants said afterwards "Our meeting was taking place in an atmosphere of assumed consensus. Had one senior adviser opposed the venture I believe Kennedy would have cancelled it. No-one spoke up." These things are all sociological factors which come into play during newspaper budget conferences (*Victims of Groupthink*, 1972, Semantic Scholar).

American economist and sociologist Thorstein Veblen highlighted another phenomenon he described as 'trained incapacity' – the inability to make any new, imaginative response because of previous bureaucratic training. Organisations face a perennial problem of balancing their own need for stability and predictability with a requirement that they respond to constant change in the social environment outside. The result can be fatal to any dynamic organisation because the minds of decision-makers tend to be dragooned and regimented.

This is the essence of Veblen's theory and it goes some way to explaining a general mood in major newspapers that avoided coverage of crime as a news subject (*The Instinct of Workmanship and the State of the Industrial Arts*, The Macmillan Company, New York, 1922).

Effectively, for a variety of reasons, crime is not news under a predetermined definition of what news is meant to be. Events unrolling on the dark streets and robberies at local drug stores have little about them that is fresh, new or different. This means they are not really genuine news in the eyes of newspaper decision-makers. Crime is seen by newspapers as a constant feature of society that is not particularly newsworthy and does not merit any special treatment.

Chapter 21
Already Obsolete

The story of police and crime reporting cannot be told without the realisation that traditional printed newspapers are already obsolete. The rise of the internet has driven a spear into the heart of the newspaper industry, undercutting its former dominance of classified advertising and destroying its news leadership – and they have been unable to find a solution. The internet is a unique information and communication matrix, a virtual shadow world that has expanded to take over every aspect of modern life no matter how large or small. It is a breeding ground for change to everything connected to human society.

Within a single generation, endless new concepts have become part of everyday life: Google, emails, websites, blogging, social media, online news, zoom, Twitter, web-based commerce, industrial and military piracy, hacking and cyber espionage. No workplace could function without the internet, no bank could exist, no company could operate in its marketplace. Social media has transformed the world into something unimaginable.

It gives the same powers to kindergarten children as it does for university graduates, leaders of nations or those who control the military-industrial complex. The internet governs all scientific research and provides a ready answer for any question on earth through search engines. But it is capable of so much more. All these new inventions can be manipulated by whoever is in control of them and this could point the way to menacing changes to the world we once knew. So in many ways, George Orwell's *1984* is becoming the new reality.

The internet is leading the world towards the brink of a future that is impossible to imagine. The effects on the print media can only be described as devastating.

Newspapers must be laboriously researched and edited, carefully laid out in pages and printed on super-fast rotary presses for delivery to news outlets and front doors each morning. But by then the world has already moved on and newspapers are out of date the moment the plates go on the presses. They can't compete with the instantaneous nature of websites, on-line newspapers, bloggers, social media, emails, and an endless stream of other inventions. They have ushered in a bonanza for emerging Silicon Valley technology, which in turn has spawned a new species of Big Tech billionaires who now dominate the entire world. And alongside this astonishing social and technological upheaval, the profession of journalism is itself under assault as the great newsrooms are depopulated and dying.

News desks everywhere are being emptied of former teams of investigative reporters, specialist writers, columnists and sub-editors. No-one could have foreseen this newspaper train wreck coming down the track.

Within a few years of the arrival of the internet, media insiders quickly noticed that traditional newspapers were losing their grip on the news cycle, but few newspapers reported what was really going on. It has continued to get worse year after year as newspaper owners explore every possible avenue to stay soluble and relevant. Most have sold off all the assets they can, cut workforces to a bare minimum and tried heroically to make on-line editions of their newspapers work. Within a few years of the arrival of websites and internet service providers, the newspaper industry began its irreversible decline.

End of an Era

In the 1960s and 1970s there was a costly transition as newspapers began moving from hot metal typesetting and letterpress printing to photocomposition and offset printing. Many thousands of printers lost their jobs once cut-and-paste was used to do page layouts. Then the onset of computer systems eventually cost the jobs of all the remaining compositors, who were retained for the initial stages to pull pages together. They were phased out very quickly as typology and page layout were constructed entirely by sub-editors using new-fangled computer software. Printing equipment was then updated with the latest rotary offset presses, which unleashed high quality colour to bring newspapers to brilliant life.

The *Saguache Crescent* from Saguache, Colorado is the last newspaper in America still produced using a Linotype hot metal typesetting machine (Wikipedia, The Saguache Crescent).

The next tsunami of newsroom casualties came down the tracks after 2000, when newspapers across the world began outsourcing sub-editing as part of cutting costs and shrinking workforces. But this removed the traditional back room of news desks where the collective wisdom of journalism had been preserved. At least half of all editorial jobs were replaced by online contractors in less than a generation. Editorial standards have been falling as newspapers struggle to fill news pages with a skeleton crew of reporters and editorial staff. This in turn has slashed the ability of newspapers to chase news or to carry out detailed investigations including crime reporting.

The internet is an ever-expanding cloud of information and communication tendrils reaching across the world instantaneously. Newspapers have no answer to this technology.

Driven by Self-Interest

Newspapers are privately-owned companies seeking to make a profit on their investment. They are not driven by a desire to foster a better understanding of the causes of crime or to change society by running campaigns. Nor are they on crusades to throw their weight behind the little man, fight oppressive government or tackle crookedness. Mostly these forces represent their advertisers anyway.

Their principal job is to get a newspaper out each day by whatever means possible. They do however traditionally seek to influence outcomes in elections by choosing sides. But often such partisan political filibustering reflects the personal alliances of owners. Thus, interest in covering any subject matter is measured in corporate terms of circulation and ledgers, profits, charts and spirals, which in turn are the real indicators of newsworthiness. If boardrooms are to satisfy shareholders on the stock exchange, then the bottom line is always profoundly economic – to sell advertising and make a profit. And this is why newspapers have been hit so hard by the internet.

State of Collapse

The American newspaper industry's total workforce fell from 427,600 employees in 1995 to 183,900 in 2016. Over this same period the number of employees in internet companies rose from 31,500 to 197,800 (Employment trends in newspaper publishing and other media, Bureau of Labour Statistics 1990–2016). National classified advertising revenue for newspapers in America plunged from $36 billion in 1995 to $16.5 billion in 2017 (Pew Research Centre Journalism & Media). Daily national circulation fell from 61,229,000 to

30,948,419 over the same 22-year period. By 2017, Sunday circulation had dropped from 58,193,000 to 33,971,695.

Newspapers have been forced to outsource non-core employees and offered redundancies to tenured staff, sell off property and assets, discard non-metro news desks, end zoning, reduce editions, offload investigative reporting teams and reduce the extent and diversity of news coverage. As early as November 1998 the *Los Angeles Times* announced cutbacks and reorganisations eliminating about 750 editorial positions (A Brief History of the Los Angeles Times).

Newspapers cannot replace the vanishing classified advertising bonanza and they have failed to compensate for shrinking circulation via on-line subscriptions at give-away prices. The bulk of advertising revenue from online editions goes to Big Tech giants like Google anyway.

Newspaper operations stayed afloat using all means at their disposal – but it was all done behind a general attitude of concealment. Newspapers usually avoid discussing their own plight and most of their readers are not told what is going on. All newspapers have set up their own on-line newspapers because it is impossible for print to ignore them and stay relevant. Online editions give access to news content for subscribers, many of whom no longer buy a real newspaper. It means newspapers can update news stories or launch breaking news online and this maintains a façade of immediacy. But it has opened the door for on-line pirates who can plunder the news content at will and who are unlikely to give any attribution.

The ability to make changes to stories across the news cycle gives newspapers little advantage. Nor are they in the forefront of breaking news anymore, a traditional advantage for well-resourced newsrooms. On-line outfits do not have the same costly overheads of newsrooms, printing presses, the cost of newsprint and maintaining distribution networks. They can operate from anywhere in low-cost premises and update news issues on a minute-by-minute basis anyway.

In a dynamic media world news is now usually built around issues largely cherry-picked from across the internet, principally the ceaseless ebb and flow of social media traffic. This is degrading the quality of news content and killing off independent investigations. It is easier to slant news coverage towards the lives of the rich and famous, political elites, celebrities or sporting heroes, who provide an endless stream of comments, usually about themselves.

Loss of Public Trust

Desperate newspapers will now give editorial support to anyone as long as they are prepared to pay for it through advertising. This has eroded the concept of journalistic independence and impartiality. It's easy to see why newspapers and the mainstream media have lost public respect and trust. Very little effort is made to provide balanced coverage of any issue, in particular politics.

No wonder people have come to distrust the media and have lost faith in newspapers of record. It's easier and more efficient to follow breaking trends, for which the internet is perfectly adapted. Media releases are a powerful new weapon because media outlets no longer bother with a balanced viewpoint or even checking for accuracy.

There are no editorial gatekeepers anymore to sort through this endless cascade of minutia, and to arrange it into some sort of order or level of importance. Increasingly, the obsession with on-line news ignores reliable sources, research, factual content and balance in news coverage. Errors or oversights are simply disregarded as new issues emerge to replace them. These considerations were once the bedrock of journalism that imposed discipline and a sense of order. Reporting staff would have their sails trimmed by sub-editors who would pore over copy and reject poor quality or wild and unsubstantiated claims.

Say Goodbye to the Age of Newspapers

Newspapers have no choice – they have to subsidise their web activities and drive readers to on-line subscriptions to retain any presence in a rapidly shrinking hard-copy market. All across America as newspaper revenues plummeted by the end of 2008, ad sales were down about 25 per cent from three years earlier. Reporter Paul Starr said – presciently as it turns out – it's time to say, "Goodbye to the age of newspapers, hello to a new era of corruption. Publishers cannot seem to shed editors, reporters and sections of their papers fast enough. And there is more pain to come. Newspapers are also shrinking in numbers of pages, breadth of news coverage, features of various kinds and home delivery of print editions," (*The New Republic*, March 2009).

The underpinning standards, morality and ethics of journalism are also under assault. The term 'fake news' has become widespread, coming into popular usage during the 2016 presidential election campaign. It defines a collapse of journalistic integrity across parts of the media and the rise of unverified pseudo-events as news. The mainstream media is now seen by a considerable section of the American public as bigoted and biased and guilty of activism on a grand scale.

But was this really to do with politics? Or was it because people had become aware of the decline in media truthfulness, balance and openness? Is it because the internet is perfect for running narratives and propaganda? There is a general perception of loss of breadth in news coverage and the substitution of opinion for straight news. Newspapers have begun to abandon the guiding discipline of journalism without saying they are doing it.

Perhaps it has something to do with the depopulation of newsrooms on a grand scale, that means they can no longer actually produce news. It seems they have no choice but to reprint press releases from advertisers. An implosion of news ethics and journalism has become the new normal without anyone realising it. This devolution of journalism has been kept quiet, perhaps hoping no-one would notice. Media errors, misreporting or deliberate deception or omissions are now noticeably rarely acknowledged in the news cycle.

Opinion and editorialising are now the new straight news and this transition away from factual reporting to opinion is a more recent phenomenon. News reporting is dominated overwhelmingly by online messages from political figures, influencers or celebrities on a vast scale. Opinion pieces from vested interests were once carefully identified and news pages were the province of actual news. But these boundaries were easily crossed once editors became captive to the economic interests of a newspaper's skittish corporate owners. At what point did comment or opinion replace news? At what point will newspapers be declared extinct?

A Knight Gallup poll in 2018 revealed that the spread of inaccurate information on the internet is now a serious problem for news coverage. Public trust in the media is at an all-time low based on the views of 73 per cent of 19,000 participants in the Knight Gallup Report, September 2018. Such widespread deep distrust of the mainstream media makes a mockery of 'newspapers of record' and the concept of journalism as a profession. It certainly raises questions about how newspapers can continue to be regarded as the Fourth Estate of Government (What is the Fourth Estate? ThoughtCo.).

Printed newspapers were at the height of their power and influence back in the early to mid-1990s. They could afford to run extra editions and promote zoning. They could still accommodate large investigative reporting teams and retain specialists like police and crime reporters. This gave newspapers unparalleled claims to news industry leadership, but those days are gone and the last generation of newspaper crime reporters is going extinct as well.

As the great flagships of the newspaper industry spiral into decay one after another the bedrock of journalism is crumbling everywhere. This is creating a different type of society as newspapers surrender their guardianship of impartiality, fairness, factual research and balanced news reporting. They are being replaced by a hybrid form of media activism driven over the internet – and the rise of unsourced opinion and comment presented as fact. But how has this come about in the world's greatest democracy in history, a fortress for freedom and defender of the right to voice an opinion? Wars have been fought over such things.

Journalism in Crisis

Newspapers have been iconic symbols of democracy and freedom since the Enlightenment, the Age of Reason and the rise of science and humanitarian ideals. But they have faced many challenges along the way as society and technology continually transform the media. They fought off the arrival of radio then took on the challenge of television, always modifying their product to retain essential shape and purpose.

Newspaper specialist Robin Bromby said newspapers had been failing for a century and they continued to do so. But Bromby said they had not found a successful formula to survive by going online. Newspapers once enjoyed the revenue referred to as 'rivers of gold' but the internet was the last straw for print news (Newspapers: a century of decline, Robin Bromby).

As Bromby explains, newspaper conglomerates amassed a fortune for decades through their dominance of the news cycle and classified advertising. But those riches were used up paying out flashy dividends to shareholders, investing in other types of media (like the use of television by the *Chicago Tribune,* which ran eight channels) and expanding news desks and the number of executives. They invested in large specialist teams of investigative reporters to drive the news.

The *Los Angeles Times* featured at least one of these lengthy investigations every day of the week in the 1990s. But nothing was put aside to provide for this reversal. No-one could have foreseen the internet because no-one can foretell the future.

One-fifth of American newspapers had shut down by 2004, according to research from the University of North Carolina. Digital news operations were growing but the number of journalism jobs in America fell 26 per cent from 2008 to 2020, according to the Pew Research Center.

'Ghost newspapers' are a symptom of the decline, the term applied to major metro dailies that are struggling with deep staff cuts that put local coverage under threat. Duke University researchers studied 16,000 news stories published in 100 communities finding that fewer than 1 in 5 had a local focus. Under half the stories were produced locally.

Newspapers admit they have been unable to respond to the rapidly worsening homicide rates that sent their cities spinning into an undeclared state of civil war from 1989. They failed to fully explain or find the causes or the remedies for the massive implosion in living conditions at the heart of all large cities. They were unable to tell the American people about the extent of the deadly impact of armed street gangs. In taking this approach they let America's political leadership off the hook, and they failed to inform the public of what was really going on – in their own self-interest.

But why should newspapers be responsible for the failings of society? Their long-standing relations with police have been at breaking point for decades and much of this was due to social forces beyond their control. Television presented crime news as a rolling series of bloody incidents without context or explanation.

By the 1990s newspapers were no longer committed to covering major crime outbreaks, and given a lack of genuine interest by political representatives, who could blame them? Their campaigns did not lead to any political intervention to address the urban questions they raised inside large cities, about nightmarish homicide rates, an explosion in illegal drugs, the rise of gangs and an increasingly violent and desperate society.

But those who should have taken action are the political elites, who have done nothing to respond, thus leaving a dark stain on American history and this is why the crisis has returned.

Newspapers once brought hope, life, energy, stability, security and culture to modern free democracies, but they are vanishing like butterflies on a summer's day. How will the disappearance of newspapers and their combined corporate knowledge and traditions affect society and what does it mean for democracy, in which the free press is a crucial part?

Journalism academic and author Margaret Simons wrote in 2017 that journalism was facing a crisis worldwide and that 'we might be entering a new dark age' (The Guardian).

"Now, partly thanks to Donald Trump, many more people are turning their mind to the future of news, including 'fake' news and its opposite. How in the future are we to know the difference between truth, myth and lies?"

Newspapers have had many perceived roles in society, as watchdogs of official corruption, defenders of democracy and the Fourth Estate of Government. These historic callings have long been part of the ideology of newspapers and journalism in a modern society. Many experienced journalists and editors felt this was part of the persona of their profession, but it was really a perception for newspaper outsiders.

Editors once made all day-to-day editorial decisions, but accountants now control the purse strings enforce editorial direction. The task of packaging the best news each day is no longer the driving force for newspapers and perhaps it never was. They seek to have become multi-interest magazine style products which provide a variety of services and entertainment to an endless array of advertisers and consumers.

They have been forced to develop on-line editions, which by and large have failed to shore up shrinking advertising revenue. Nor have they found an answer to the instantaneous nature of social media, the fact is their product is now old news once papers are delivered the next day.

Survival strategies include a greater reliance on national media networking to help patch together each day's news budget and to broaden on-line subscriptions. None of that has worked. Breaking news stories now come as part of on-going narratives, enabling newspapers to milk issues for a few extra days. Newspapers all struggle to carry out news gathering due to the skeleton workforces in largely boutique-style newsrooms. They have limited scope for research or investigative journalism.

The shrinkage of editorial teams has forced newspapers to depend more than ever on opinion-based content instead of straight reporting. They are forced to rely on media networks to sustain on-going narratives built around politics, the economy or other trending issues. Newspaper businesses are more than willing to 'partner' with advertisers by reproducing media releases as news. Local news coverage is dying everywhere and there is little incentive to partner with police to report on crime.

This is no longer traditional journalism. It reflects a massive shift in the nature of newspapers in an on-line world that has all but destroyed its capacity to profit from classified advertising. Basically, they are just doing the best they can to stay afloat in an endlessly shifting global culture that changes by the day.

They are involved in the fight of their lives in an on-line world that no longer cares much what they do one way or another. They have become obsolete, and the descent into opinion and running thinly veiled advertising as news means they have become pariahs instead of news leaders.

All they have left are their iconic mastheads, a last link to the barnstorming battles of the broadsheets.